# Clyde Walcott

Manchester University Press

# Global Icons

# Clyde Walcott

## Statesman of West Indies cricket

Peter Mason

Manchester University Press

Published by Manchester University Press
Oxford Road, Manchester, M13 9PL
www.manchesteruniversitypress.co.uk

British Library Cataloguing-in-Publication Data
A catalogue record for this book is available from the British Library

ISBN 978 1 5261 8160 2 hardback
ISBN 978 1 5261 6975 4 paperback

First published 2024

The publisher has no responsibility for the persistence or accuracy of
URLs for any external or third-party internet websites referred to in
this book, and does not guarantee that any content on such websites
is, or will remain, accurate or appropriate.

Typeset by Newgen Publishing UK

# Contents

# Figures

# Acknowledgements

Many thanks to the Society of Authors Foundation for providing financial support to help with the writing and research of this book.

I'm also grateful to Michael Holding, Ian McDonald, Reds Perreira, Brian Scovell and Jack Simmons for talking to me about Clyde Walcott, and to Brigid Meadows for her assistance on my writing 'retreat' at St Ethelwold's House in Abingdon.

# Introduction

The cricket writer and commentator John Arlott occasionally liked to tell the story of a local miner nervously seeking out Clyde Walcott in the changing room at the Chesterfield pavilion in 1950 when the West Indies were playing Derbyshire on their tour of England.

> 'Mr Walcott, my name is also Walcott and I wondered if by any chance we might be related?' he said. Clyde Walcott stared friendlily at the man without being able to find the words to broach this interesting prospect, when a voice behind him said: 'Don't stand for that Clyde, man, tell him you're pure African, brother, pure African.' If the Derbyshire miner was disappointed at having hopes of ancestral links dashed, his nerves and seriousness gradually disappeared as he was given several large rums, departing an hour or so later a West Indies fan.[1]

That story, whether apocryphal or not, neatly encapsulates the charm and appeal of Clyde Walcott, as well as his lasting significance in terms of race relations in cricket and beyond. A firm believer in standing up for what he was, rather than what people thought he ought to be, Walcott was an outspoken advocate of his racial identity, and of his place in society. But he was also a highly accomplished diplomat, gifted with the ability to make his point in such a thoughtful and conciliatory manner that interlocutors were generally sent away not only with a much better understanding of his perspective but with a lasting sense of admiration and respect. A quiet, sometimes stern-looking man, he was nonetheless more than capable of having good fun and, as with the faltering Derbyshire miner, was accustomed to turning an awkward situation to everyone's advantage.

Barbadian by birth but a world citizen by operation, Sir Clyde Walcott was one of the greatest cricketers of all time and a legend of the game. For the West Indies in the 1950s he was part of the formidable 'three Ws', a batting triumvirate of Weekes, Worrell and Walcott that helped to reconfigure West Indies cricket by providing it with an identity that was separate from, and in many ways opposed to, its colonial past. At a time when cricket in the Caribbean fed into the nationalist struggle for independence, he helped for the first time to establish the West Indies as a world force in the game, taking part in the lobbying and campaigning that eventually led to Worrell's appointment as the first black captain of the team.

Simultaneously, one of Walcott's most important contributions to social and racial change was his work in British Guiana (now Guyana) as a cricket and social welfare organiser for the country's vast sugar estates. In that role between 1954 and 1970 he made massive strides in the development of cricket among poor, mainly Indo-Guyanese plantation workers, widening access to the game, upgrading facilities, organising clubs and competitions and improving coaching techniques. This led directly to the emergence of a number of world-class Indo-Guyanese cricketers – including Rohan Kanhai and Joe Solomon – from a tiny area of the Caribbean that had hitherto been unknown and overlooked. In the process, and given the importance of cricket in the Caribbean, Walcott helped to bring new self-belief and a greater sense of belonging to hundreds of thousands of people of Indian extraction across the region.

After retiring from Test cricket, Walcott became a globally prominent cricket administrator for the West Indies from the late 1960s to the early 1990s, playing a crucial role in developing the proud spirit and consciousness of teams under Clive Lloyd and Viv Richards that ruled the world for more than a decade and gave a huge boost to the image of the Caribbean and its diaspora. A vocal supporter of using cricket to apply pressure on the South African apartheid regime, in 1993 he became chairman of the International Cricket Council – the first black man to hold that position – and went on to shake up the organisation by throwing off the shackles of the traditional rulers of the game, England and Australia.

Despite those many achievements, Walcott remained a modest and softly spoken man, unspoiled by the trappings of fame, committed to putting back into cricket – and society – what he felt he had received in return. Often that unassuming demeanour meant that the extent of his influence was downplayed. This first biography aims to shine a brighter light on his understated but deeply important role in effecting change through the vehicle of cricket.

# Early years – and first-class cricket

Family legend has it that the midwife who brought Clyde Leopold Walcott into the world on 17 January 1926 at his parents' house in Bridgetown, Barbados, was also present at the home births of his future pals and fellow cricketing superstars Everton Weekes and Frank Worrell.

The midwife's name has been lost to history, and of course the legend might not be true. But it seems entirely plausible that she would have ministered at all three births, given that each baby was born within the same square mile and within a time span of just 18 months.

That one woman was at hand to deliver a collection of incontrovertible greats of cricket – the 'three Ws' of global fame – seems scarcely believable. And yet they would all have been born on her patch, and she could easily have spread a metaphorical baby's blanket over the lot of them.

True or false, the idea that Worrell, Weekes and Walcott might have shared a midwife throws into relief the extraordinary fact of their mutual co-existence – that a triumvirate of such magnificent cricketers, all batting in the middle order for the West Indies, could have emerged from exactly the same place at exactly the same time. It's a circumstance that surely will never be repeated, no matter how long the game is played.

Walcott, of course, became used to being bracketed with the other two Ws wherever he went – and was happy for that to be the case. But he was a great cricketer in his own right, and would have stood tall in the game even if Worrell and Weekes had never existed. More than that, he went on to create his own series of notable achievements in other areas of life.

Despite the proximity of their birth, Walcott was not to meet Worrell until they both arrived at the same secondary school at the age of 11, and there was no encounter with Weekes until several years after that. All three, however, shared a common space in Bridgetown, and it was their destiny to live intertwined lives.

Walcott's father, Frank, was an engineer at the print works of the daily Barbados *Advocate* newspaper, and his mother, Ruth, who claimed to have Scottish blood (hence the name Clyde), was a church-going Methodist housewife. With his brother, Keith, who was two years older, Clyde first lived with his parents in a sizeable rented house that had once been a sugar plantation manager's residence, in the New Orleans area of Bridgetown on the corner of Baxter's Road and Westbury Road, not far from the Kensington Oval cricket ground. However, they also shared the place with 'various uncles and an aunt',[1] often up to four at a time.

One of those uncles, Ernest, had been a co-founder of the locally famous Empire cricket club; another, Harold, was a prominent umpire; and Clyde's father, too, was a cricket enthusiast – hardly a rarity on an island that was mad about the sport. Barbados, though only 166 square miles, smaller in area than Luxembourg and, at Walcott's birth, with a population of around 200,000, has long been a cricketing hotbed that has punched above its weight.

A more or less perfect place for cricket, it has hard, true pitches based on coral and sedimentary rock that have proved ideal for nurturing fast bowlers and free-hitting batsman, as well as a hot but agreeably moderate tropical climate that interferes only mildly with the playing of the game. Densely peopled, compact and generally low lying, travelling around the island is easy, allowing for a thriving club cricket scene with a high concentration of domestic clubs, while it has also had a relatively stable economic and social history compared to other parts of the former British West Indies. From 1627 until independence in 1966, Barbados experienced more than 400 unbroken years of direct British control, allowing cricket to lay down deep roots.

Clyde's first encounter with the sport was at the age of three, when he was presented by his father with a cut-down bat for use in the large backyard of the family house, a big enough space to attract a revolving daily cast of players from the local neighbourhood. 'There were not just boys playing in our backyard, but men, some of them leading cricketers from the club sides', he recalled.[2] 'There was a galvanized fence around the yard and we also used a piece of galvanized steel as the stumps. You knew if you were out because the ball would hit the metal with a loud twang. For most of my childhood years we played for five or six hours a day until it became dark.'[3]

When the family later moved to the Black Rock area of Bridgetown to a larger property, they found themselves with an even bigger parcel of attached land, increasing the number of people who were able to join in. During the appropriate season the yard was occasionally turned over to football, and the boys also enjoyed regular bike rides on the weekend after Sunday school, as well as trips to the cinema. But for the most part cricket reigned supreme.

In primary school Clyde demonstrated far more interest in physical activities than his studies, although he was a bright enough pupil. At home the adult atmosphere was vibrant and thought provoking but hardly studious, and the only book he recalled tackling from cover to cover as a youngster was a short biography of the great Australian cricketer Don Bradman. 'We spent far more time debating and arguing than we did reading', he said.[4] 'When it was dark and supper was finished, the uncles and aunts would join us to talk about the issues of the day, the state of West Indian cricket, the latest political crisis, or whatever took our fancy. Sometimes the exchanges became heated, but it was a way of learning about people and events. That is the West Indian way.'[5]

It was, by the standards of the black population in Barbados at the time, a comfortable middle-class upbringing with enough money from his father's job, and contributions from the wider family, to ensure that both boys did not go wanting. Clyde was inclined to be the more demanding and troublesome of the two, though never badly behaved on any spectacular scale, while Keith was more self-contained and polite.

Typically, while Keith passed the scholarship exam for entry into the state-run but fee-paying Combermere School, Clyde failed his test in 1937, and so his parents decided to pay the eight dollars a term to allow him to join his brother – a sum of money that would have been well beyond the means of most black Barbadians at the time.

Combermere, dating back to 1695, was one of the three leading secondary schools in Barbados, each based around the 'muscular learning' principles of the British public school system, with its emphasis on the classics and sporting endeavour, each of them, according to Keith Sandiford, an authority on Barbadian schooling, 'making a significant contribution to the development of the cricket cult in Barbados'.[6]

The other two top institutions, Harrison College and The Lodge, were a notch above Combermere in the social pecking order, and as such were favoured by the white elite who made up around 10 per cent of the population. As a result, Combermere laid rather more emphasis on practical schooling for the black middle-class pupils whose parents had sent them there to gather employability skills.

In his first year Clyde made an immediate impact in cricket at Combermere by moving straight into the first XI at the age of 12 – in a team mainly made up of 16-, 17- and 18-year-olds, as well as some masters. The school, along with Harrison College and The Lodge, was allowed to compete in the first division of the main Barbados league, which meant that Walcott was also pitched in against fully grown and highly proficient adult club cricketers from the island's best sides. As one of the youngest players ever to appear in the league, and not yet possessed of the solid build or commanding physical presence that he boasted in later years, Walcott's promise was more noticeable than his effectiveness. 'I had no strokes to speak of in those days: I would take half an hour to score six or seven runs', he said.[7] But the experience was invaluable.

Entry into the first XI also allowed Walcott to meet Worrell, who was in the year above him at Combermere. Although Worrell's biographer, Ivo

Tennant, claims that 'they did not get on particularly well'[8] at that stage, Worrell was later happy to declare that 'from the very earliest days Clyde and I have been buddies',[9] and it is reasonable to assume that a friendship of sorts developed. Whatever transpired, the two were parted within a couple of years when, at the age of 14 in 1940, Walcott's parents paid for him to move over to Harrison College, along with Keith. The fees there were a much more significant undertaking for the family, especially as the recent advent of the Second World War had rendered the general economic situation much tighter, even in Barbados.

'We were just beginning to feel the pinch of war in those days, though I must say that we were very lucky to get away with it as lightly as we did', Walcott said.[10] 'There were some shortages: rice, the basic ingredient of our diet, imported meat, butter and flour were all tight and – worst of all, it seemed to a 14-year-old boy – English cricket gear was hard to obtain.'[11]

Clyde found that the quality of cricket at Harrison College was of a greater order than at Combermere, but his parents had sent him there to improve his academic performance rather than his sporting prowess; in particular, they were keen to see him follow in Uncle Ernest's footsteps by becoming a dentist.

While Clyde did just enough to keep himself out of academic trouble, however, he continued to show little interest in anything other than sport. An accomplished footballer who later represented Barbados, he was also a top performer on the athletics field in the long jump, hurdles and high jump, winning the Victor Ludorum as best all-round athlete in track and field events in two successive years. He was also an excellent tennis and table tennis player. But it was cricket that held his main attention.

In the Harrison College first XI, under the captaincy of his brother, Clyde initially went through a bad run of form with the bat. Worried that he might lose his place, he decided to add to his value by taking up wicketkeeping. The ploy worked, and he became a star player in the side for the rest of his time there. Thus properly established, however, he dropped his wicket-keeping in favour of bowling useful inswingers.

With an upright batting style and great poise at the crease, Walcott gave the impression that he had been well coached, but he always denied this was the case, pointing out that even at Harrison College there was no technical instruction to speak of, beyond a general injunction to 'keep playing well forward, with the left elbow well up'.[12]

As with Combermere, Harrison College also played in the Barbados League first division, in which Clyde opened the batting while Keith followed lower down at No. 4 or No. 5. During the 1941 season Clyde hit 500 runs in ten innings for the school, including three centuries, and on the basis of that fine form he was called up to play for Barbados, along with Worrell and Keith, in two first-class matches against Trinidad in early 1942.

Walcott had to borrow the necessary kit from his school – he never owned a pair of pads until he played Test cricket – and to celebrate the landmark his father presented him with his first proper bat, which broke in the nets before he even had a chance to use it properly. The first match in Port of Spain began on the day of his sixteenth birthday in January 1942, making him the youngest player ever to have been chosen for Barbados. In front of a crowd of 16,000, on an unfamiliar coconut matting wicket (as opposed to the grass wickets of Barbados), he opened up in the first innings with George Carew, scoring just 8 before batting at No. 4 in the second and faring even worse with a duck. Shortly afterwards an outbreak of tonsillitis laid him up in the team's old wooden guest house, the Hotel de Paris, forcing him to miss the second match – although it was a moot point as to whether he would have been selected in any case.

Regardless of that inauspicious start, faith in Walcott's young talent was strong enough for him to be picked for two further matches against Trinidad in July that year, his selection eased by an injury to Keith, which freed up a place in the side for the first match in Bridgetown. This time Walcott proved his worth, compiling 70 at No. 7 in the only Barbados innings of the first encounter and then making 67 and 50 at No. 3 in the second, also in Bridgetown.

By now, despite his parents' doubts, Walcott was certain where his future lay – and it would not be in dentistry. In October 1944, while still at school, he scored his first century for Barbados, an untypically circumspect 125 batting at No. 3 in a timeless match in Georgetown on a four-match tour of British Guiana. From that point onwards he rarely considered any other path than a life in top-line cricket, although given the financial state of the game in the West Indies he knew he would also have to work in other spheres to make a living.

When he left Harrison College in 1944 at the age of 18, Walcott had failed every exam he had taken; there was not a certificate to his name. As a Harrison old boy, however, and perhaps thanks to contacts through his family, he managed to secure a job as a clerk to a local geologist, taking instrument readings and running errands as his employer carried out an exhaustive survey of the water supply in Barbados. It was an easy enough post to hold down, gave time off to play cricket when needed, and proved to be a firm foundation on which to concentrate on his sporting career across the next two years. It also, for the first time, provided Walcott with some measure of monetary freedom, allowing him to experience the novelties of going out dancing and meeting young women.

Once school cricket was over, Walcott joined the Bridgetown-based Spartan club, of which his brother was already a member. Cricket teams in Barbados, in line with much of the rest of society, were arranged more or less along racial and class lines, with the

Pickwick and Wanderers clubs reserved as bastions of the white population. Pickwick had been formed in response to the exclusivity of the Wanderers, and in turn Spartan had been set up in 1893 as a haven for black and mixed-race players. Over the years, however, Spartan had often refused entry to various 'socially inferior' cricketers, until in 1914 a rival black working-class club, Empire, was formed. Given that most of Walcott's family had previously been members of Empire, his accession to Spartan was a notable indicator of the raised social status of his parents. Though he would later become more sensitive to concerns around race and class, at this stage, it seems, he was more concerned with what Spartan could offer him, including a sporting social life that included tennis and table tennis with a new set of friends.

At Spartan, Walcott settled into a style of play that became a hallmark for the rest of his career: bold, forceful and hard-hitting. By now more or less up to the full 6ft 2in of his adult height and already developing the muscular physique of a heavyweight boxer, it was his strength that immediately drew the attention; in particular, his fiercely punched back-foot drives and exhilarating hook shots, which he would often execute standing on tiptoe to make full use of his height. With a short, right-handed grip on the bat handle, he loved to take on fast bowling. But allied to the power, there was a surety of technique that allowed him to defend stoutly when circumstances required, and he played with supreme control even when on the rampage.

In January 1945, aged 19, Walcott was back in Trinidad for another short tournament, during which he had his first encounter, in the first match, with Everton Weekes, who had been picked for his Barbados debut after a period away on military service. With Worrell in the team, this was also the first time the three Ws played together in the same XI, although no one yet knew the significance of that moment. By the beginning of the following year Walcott had also taken on wicketkeeping duties for Barbados in succession to Stanton Gittens, despite not having stood behind the stumps since his early school days – or even having fulfilled that role for Spartan.

Matters progressed increasingly well, if reasonably quietly, until soon after his twentieth birthday, when Walcott thrust himself into the global spotlight with an extraordinary innings of 314 not out – the highest score of his first-class career – against Trinidad in Port of Spain in February 1946. In doing so he not only beat the highest score by a Barbadian (304 not out by Percy Tarilton) but compiled an unbeaten five-hour stand of 574 runs for the fourth wicket with Worrell, who scored 255 not out – a world record for any partnership at the time and still the highest West Indian partnership for any wicket.

It was Walcott's first real taste of life in the limelight. 'The press gave it all they had. Headlines, photographs, interviews … we were in a whirl', he said.[13] '[The] deluge of cables from our families and friends had to be seen to be believed. For a boy of 20 it was all a bit intoxicating.'[14]

Around the same time Walcott had managed to secure a better paid job as a clerk with his brother's employer, the Control Office, a government body that supervised the wartime rationing of food and petrol in Barbados. Shortly afterwards, on the back of their magnificent stand, Walcott and Worrell were invited to visit New York to play in a series of lucrative exhibition matches for the Caribbean expatriate community there, at the Randle's Island Stadium. When his employers refused Walcott time off for the all-expenses-paid tour, he decided, against the advice of his parents, to throw in the job and risk all. 'I worked out that I could save more during my three months' trip to America than I would be able to in two years in my office job', he said.[15] 'As to security – what boy of 20-odd gives it a thought, unless he has to? By this time I was buoyed up by an unshakable confidence that I was going to make the grade in big cricket.'[16]

The trip to the US was a fairly lengthy one that encompassed the whole of the short American cricket season from July to September, and it was Walcott's first time away from the Caribbean. Despite the strange surroundings he was able to stave off homesickness by staying with cousins in New York, as well as for periods with Worrell's mother, Grace, who had emigrated to Brooklyn some years before. Nonetheless, it was a culture shock. 'My first impression ... was that everyone there was crazy', he said.[17] 'I just could not begin to understand the speed at which they lived their lives. Fast cars, clanging trains, screaming brakes, tall buildings and express elevators ... it was all new to me.'[18]

The cricket in the US was not always of the highest quality, but the financial side of the equation was certainly to Walcott's liking. There would be collections among the crowd every time he achieved something of note – even hit a six – and on one occasion a spectator rushed out to the wicket to stuff a ten-dollar bill in his pocket after he had knocked a ball out of the ground. He returned to Barbados with an appreciable sum of money – and as a welcome bonus was able to apply for, and secure, another job with the Control Office at a higher salary.

The American trip cemented Walcott's new friendship with Worrell, and in March 1947 Weekes was drawn more firmly into their orbit as the three of them went to Jamaica with Barbados for two matches in Kingston, where they had fun together off the field as well as on it. Soon Walcott and Worrell were back in New York for more exhibition matches, only this time with the addition of Weekes.

As before, Clyde had to resign his job at the Control Office – a move that finally burnt his bridges there. But again the US trip was financially rewarding, and in any case the blow of having to leave his employment for a second time was cushioned just before he left, when he was offered – and accepted – a more flexible job selling insurance in Barbados for a Canadian firm. By now his profile had reached the point where his new employers, at least, realised the potential benefit of having him on their payroll.

On his first trip to America Walcott had been blissfully unaware of racial tensions in the US, at least on a face-to-face basis. But on his second journey he experienced his first taste of the colour bar. Travelling with a small group of black West Indian players to New York by plane, he disembarked for a change of flight at Miami airport in the southern state of Florida, where, hungry after a night of travel, he and his companions went looking for breakfast. Once they had found a suitable restaurant, they parked themselves at the nearest available table, only to be told that it was for whites only, and that they would have to move to the back.

Barbados, though a racially stratified society, had nothing so obvious in the way of segregation, and the instruction came as a shock to Walcott and his young friends. 'The whole thing disgusted and sickened us', he said.[19] 'Of course we had heard of these things, but they had never happened to us before.' Noting that the table to which he was directed had no linen or other frills, he also observed that his entourage was 'served with the same food as everyone else, and we paid for it with the same money'[20] – yet were treated as second-class citizens by dint of their colour.

> What made matters worse was the thought, which came to me then, that we, as cricketers, were much better off than most of our race. People – at any rate, those who were interested in sport – tended to accept us more readily. The pages of Wisden don't mention a man's colour. But the plight of the millions of our race who have no special abilities to single them out is a terrible thing.[21]

Reluctant to cause a scene in a foreign land, Walcott and his party ate their meal with greatly reduced appetites before leaving as soon as they could. The incident had a lasting effect on him, and served to sharpen his now burgeoning awareness of issues around race and class.

Returning to begin his insurance job after the second New York trip, Walcott had to wait until January 1948 for his next first-class matches with Barbados, two home fixtures against the touring England side – known then as MCC when playing matches outside of Tests.

In the first match Walcott posted 120 in his only innings, and though he made less of an impact in the second, with 10 and 12 not out, he had already done more than enough to justify a call-up for his first West Indies cap in the upcoming Test against England at Bridgetown. Having just turned 22, he was ready to make a start on what would turn out to be one of the most notable of all international cricketing careers.

## 2

# West Indies hero

Walcott's West Indies debut came four days after his twenty-second birthday, on 21 January 1948 at Kensington Oval. A nervous debutant, he was hardly handed the easiest of starts, as an injury crisis forced him to open the batting. His more experienced opening partner, the Trinidadian Jeff Stollmeyer, insisted on batting at No. 2, and so Walcott had to take the first ball of the match, from Maurice Tremlett.

The rain-affected pitch took spin; England gave an early spell to the young off-break bowler Jim Laker, who was also making his Test debut, and Walcott managed only eight runs before the Yorkshireman got his wicket. In the second innings of the drawn match he fared slightly better with 16, but it was a low-key beginning, made only slightly more palatable by a decent performance as wicketkeeper.

Across the four Tests of the series Walcott did not fare well with the bat, his best score coming much lower down the order at No. 8 in the final match in Jamaica, where he made 45. Mustering only 133 runs in seven innings and shifting around the order, he kept his place largely due to his wicketkeeping skills, which improved markedly as the series progressed and which delivered 16 dismissals, including five stumpings. By contrast, the other two Ws, making their own first appearances for the West Indies, were able to make more substantial contributions as the West Indies cruised to a 2–0 series victory.

Walcott was all the more frustrated at his lack of batting impact given that England had left some of their best players – including the opening bowler Alec Bedser – at home, thinking they could get away with resting them ahead of the home Ashes series later that year. 'In those colonial days we had the impression in the West Indies that the English thought they were superior and considered they "knew it all" ',[1] he said, adding that the England selectors quickly learned a 'stern lesson'.[2] The tourists failed to win a single match on the trip.

The West Indies, though, had their own selectorial failings, and these were exposed to Walcott for the first time at close hand. Unwilling to appoint the outstanding black Jamaican batsman George Headley as permanent captain for the entire series – even though he was the natural candidate for the job – the West Indies Cricket Board of Control opted for the convoluted option of selecting him to lead in just the first and fourth Tests, with the other two given over to white players, John Goddard and Stollmeyer. Headley played in the first Test but then developed a back injury which Walcott took to be an indication of his 'distaste for playing under the captaincy of Stollmeyer and Goddard'.[3] In fact, he played no further part in the series, and the surrounding intrigue gave Walcott a taste of the racial controversy that was to plague the West Indies captaincy for the rest of his international career – not least in terms of his own later claims to the job.

Despite the personal disappointments of the series, he also learned much in the new, rarefied environment

**Figure 2.1** Clyde Walcott. PA Images/Alamy Stock Photo.

of Test cricket. Off the field he was able to socialise with some of the England players, including in Trinidad, where the second Test coincided with the great spectacle of carnival. He struck up a lasting friendship with Laker and became an admirer of Godfrey Evans, not just for his wicketkeeping – which he studied closely – but for his *joie de vivre*, which he felt was West Indian in nature. Len Hutton, however, he found to be 'quiet and clam-like, with a disturbing habit of looking at opponents out of the corner of his eye'.[4]

In general, the series whetted Walcott's appetite for international cricket, so he was pleased to be picked for the West Indies' first ever tour of India later that year, which lasted from November 1948 to February 1949.

The initial leg of the journey, by boat, took Walcott for the first time to England, where during a short stop-off before the ongoing passage to India he engaged in a quick tour of the London sights, including Buckingham Palace. Expecting the tumult and mayhem he had experienced in New York, he was pleasantly surprised by the general air of calm in London, and was 'impressed by the way everything seemed to be under control – much more so than in America'.[5]

Although the cold, rainy October weather was not to his liking, Walcott was soon to be pining for it when he arrived in India, where the searing heat was unlike anything he had experienced in the Caribbean. During a warm-up match against Indian Universities at the Brabourne Stadium in Bombay (Mumbai), in which he compiled a century, Walcott was so overheated by the end of the innings that he was barely aware of what he was doing, collapsing at tea in a crying heap in the dressing room, before retiring hurt on 103.

India, which had just gone through partition, also provided Walcott with a profound culture shock. 'You could not help being struck by the appalling contrast between the vast wealth and the dreadful poverty which existed there', he said.[6] In particular, he was haunted by the sight of people living in gutters, on the pavements and in railway stations, often in the greatest poverty imaginable.

Travelling around the country by train was an uncomfortable and dirty experience, the hotels were terrible, there was little in the way of a social life to keep the players entertained, and, hand on heart, Walcott was unable to say that he actually enjoyed the trip. The cricket, too, was sometimes dull and unsatisfactory, with a preponderance of draws across all the tour matches and only one of the five Tests producing a result.

Nonetheless, the West Indies won the series 1–0 and the tour was a great personal success for Walcott, who scored 152 in the first Test in Delhi (his maiden century), putting on 267 for the fourth wicket with Gerry Gomez, a West Indies record for any wicket in Tests at the time. Following up with 108 in the third Test in Calcutta (Kolkata), he finished with 452 runs across the five Tests at an average of 64.57 and had the highest aggregate of any player on the trip – 1,366 – while also picking up 27 dismissals behind the stumps. At the back end of the tour he made a century in one of two first-class fixtures against Ceylon (now Sri Lanka) (a country he liked better than India), and earlier on he had played against the nascent Pakistan side, which had not yet been granted Test status.

Although it was only his second series with the West Indies and he had still only played nine Tests, by the end of the tour Walcott felt he belonged in Test cricket and that he had established himself in the side. 'It had also been a turning point – a maturing – in my life', he reflected. 'I had gone to India as a very inexperienced young man ... but now I felt much more sure of myself.'[7] The only downside to the tour was that he started smoking, partly to pass the time on the slow train journeys, but also because he had been presented by an admirer in Bombay with a cigarette case, which he thought he should use. The habit held on to him for the next 30 years.

Returning home to his insurance job, Walcott played just two first-class matches over the next year or so, maintaining his good form with 211 for Barbados against British Guiana in February 1950 and continuing to turn out regularly at the weekends for Spartan.

He was therefore in good nick for his next Test challenge, a four-match series in England that turned out to be the most triumphant yet for West Indies cricket. Travelling in April 1950, Walcott arrived to discover that the British newspapers had for the first time come up with the 'three Ws' tag. Given that Worrell was batting at No. 3, Weekes at 4 and Walcott at 5, it was too good to resist, and although Walcott initially felt he didn't deserve to be bracketed with the other two, it was by no means an arbitrary grouping, or based purely on alliteration. By that time the trio – aged 26, 25 and 24 respectively – had collectively begun to make a sizeable impression on the cricketing world, and it was a reasonable expectation that they would play a significant part in deciding the result of the upcoming series.

Worrell had been absent from the India tour due to a personal dispute with the West Indies Cricket Board of Control over money and disciplinary issues, so had played only three Tests to the nine each of Walcott and Weekes. But he was averaging 147 at that point and had not yet failed at the batting crease. Weekes had delivered some truly spectacular performances in India, scoring five consecutive centuries in the Tests, and Walcott, with his added value as a wicket-keeper, was now widely considered a great player in the making.

Of the three, Worrell – medium height, lithe, slim and languid – was the most naturally talented, a graceful caresser of the ball with wonderful timing and dazzling footwork, slightly less effective against fast bowling but the best against the moving ball. Weekes, tigerish, stocky and the shortest of the trio, was perhaps the most complete batsman, excellent in all conditions and against all types of bowlers, with a renowned square cut and whippy pull. Walcott, bear-like, intimidating and imposing at 15 stone, was the most devastating, a thumper of the ball who had an unusual double back-lift that encouraged some bowlers, mistakenly, to feel they could sneak the ball through his defences before his bat came down. He was probably the best of the three on a good pitch, able to pierce the inner field through sheer power, though he used a very light bat by modern standards, just two pounds and five ounces in weight.

The three Ws' personalities were markedly different, too – such that, as the Trinidadian journalist B. C. Pires has said, 'the contrasts between them were always part of their fascination for connoisseurs'.[8]

Worrell had the most obvious personal charm, which he later harnessed to become a charismatic and shrewd leader. But he was also the most wilful of the three, prone to instances of poor judgement in his early days and much more likely to challenge the status quo, sometimes getting into trouble for doing so. Weekes and Walcott, by contrast, were more consistently level-headed and rather more inclined to keep their counsel during times of potential conflict, even if they might agree with some of Worrell's stances in private. Walcott, in particular, preferred to apply his natural diplomatic skills to any situation, prompting C. L. R. James to observe that 'he cannot by any stretch of fact or imagination be called a cricketing Bolshevik'.[9]

Weekes was outgoing in the same vein as Worrell, a chatty, smiling presence who was quick to laugh and the most humorous of the three, often favouring crude jokes and banter. Though no less friendly, Walcott was rather more reserved, impassive and self-contained, and according to Michael Manley 'had an almost mournful countenance, [so that] in repose an onlooker might have thought him sad'.[10] He, too, had a sharp sense of humour, though it tended towards the cutting and sardonic. 'Wally was a great leg-puller', said Stollmeyer; 'Few escaped his scathing tongue and woe betide [anyone] who did not accept his teasing in the spirit in which it was given.'[11] Worrell noted that 'if there is a practical joke, he will be in it, and he is quite willing to have practical jokes pulled on him – but if you play a practical joke on Walcott you must expect reprisals!'[12]

None of the three Ws had excelled academically in their early years, preoccupied as they were with sport. But each had a natural intelligence that allowed them to take up studies later, and to progress in new careers. Weekes, however, was more content with a simpler life outside cricket, and arguably less ambitious, happy, later on, to remain for the most part in Barbados, while the other two pursued interests in other territories.

Each of the three 'loved each other, and were like brothers',[13] says the journalist Brian Scovell, who spent many hours in their company over the years. Walcott and Weekes were the tighter of the two – 'we were close friends, sharing a room whenever it was possible', said Weekes[14] – while Walcott and Worrell never reached quite the same state of intimacy. Worrell's biographer, Ivo Tennant, goes as far as saying that for much of the time Worrell and Walcott didn't get on at all, suggesting that this may have been due to an underlying clash of ambitions and egos, especially in the sphere of captaincy.

What Worrell and Walcott had in common, however, was their comfortable background and education. Weekes, from the Pickwick Gap district of Bridgetown, grew up poor, had an inferior education and was far more remote from the quasi-public school influences that his friends were exposed to. Nonetheless, all three had easily absorbed the Barbadian version of the English code of behaviour and were protective of its tenets. Their public behaviour was always impeccably courteous and their sense of fair play strong.

Despite any minor tensions they may have exhibited off the field, all three also deeply respected each other's talents and nearly always presented a united public front. 'In any arguments about pay, conditions and status, the Board of Control did not often succeed in its attempts to divide the three Ws', says Simon Lister.[15] 'Any tension between them probably arose from their all feeling well qualified to lead West Indies [as well as] the particular circumstances of the period,

when Test cricket became a grind and the responsibilities of the popular hero a burden.'[16]

While the three Ws were the centre of early season
attention, the surprise package for the West Indies
in England turned out to be the combination of two
unknown and untested spinners, Sonny Ramadhin
from Trinidad and Alf Valentine from Jamaica, who
were the linchpins of the subsequent 3–1 victory
across what was the West Indies' first four-match
series in England.

Ram and Val took 59 of the 77 England wickets that
fell in the Tests, and Ramadhin, in particular, had the
home batsmen bamboozled with his bewildering array
of deliveries. As the wicketkeeper, Walcott fortunately
had no problems in 'picking' Ram's subtle changes in
hand and delivery action, having worked them out
during a couple of early practice sessions in the nets.
He did, however, find that the concentration required
to keep to both bowlers, allied to the demands of
batting in the middle order, was tiring work.

The spinning pair's greatest triumph was the role
they played in the 'Victory Test', the West Indies' first
ever win against England in England. Taking 18 of the
20 wickets to fall in that second Test at Lord's, the
fabled home of cricket, they contributed to what was
the most significant landmark in West Indies cricket
up to that point, a staging post of huge psychological
importance that reverberated around the Caribbean
and inspired the famous calypso, 'Cricket Lovely

Cricket',[17] with its tribute to 'those little pals of mine, Ramadhin and Valentine'.

The calypso also reported that 'Walcott licked them around', for aside from the spin twins' key contribution, it was he who played one of the most significant roles in the West Indies' finest hour, scoring a typically belligerent 168 not out in their second innings that put the game beyond the home side and provided the platform for Ram and Val to dismiss England for 274 all out. Walcott's magnificent innings, with 24 fours, was at the time the highest score by a West Indies player in Tests in England, and proved to be a crucial intervention, tipping the scales decisively in the West Indies' favour.

'We lost some early wickets a good deal quicker than we should have done before Gerry Gomez joined me in the middle', Walcott remembered.[18] 'We decided that I should go for the bowling, while Gerry kept the other end going more solidly – in fact, that both of us should play our natural game.' The plan worked perfectly, and thanks to Walcott's century, which the great cricket journalist E. W. Swanton ranked as one of the most memorable innings he had ever seen, the West Indies were able to declare on 425 for six, setting England 601 to win. It was a target they never looked like reaching, and when their innings ended, the West Indies had won by 326 runs.

'This was our greatest moment, the occasion for which West Indies cricket had waited and worked, hoped and prayed, for so long', Walcott said. 'We had beaten England – in England. And, wonder of wonders, the victory had come at the great Lord's itself … we were drunk with pleasure even before we reached the dressing room.'[19]

Walcott rarely took much in the way of drink, but in the immediate aftermath of victory, as ecstatic West Indies fans danced around on the Lord's turf, he and Allan Rae, the other West Indies centurion in the match, gulped down a flute of champagne each, before smashing the glasses onto the floor. Captain Goddard, who ran a distillery business in Barbados, opened a crate of Goddard's Gold Braid rum he had brought over for a special occasion, and the party began.

At such a momentous juncture, Walcott's thoughts turned to his parents, for he felt vindicated in going against their wishes by focusing on cricket, yet grateful for their eventual support. However, while there was eventually to be a £150 bonus at the end of the tour, Walcott, like his teammates, was engaged for the West Indies on an amateur basis, and with just £5 a week in the form of an expenses allowance, he could not afford to ring home to celebrate.

Since 1928, as John Arlott had noted, visiting West Indies sides had been regarded by English cricket watchers as 'somewhat naive; sometimes spectacular, but never commanding'.[20] No longer would that be the case. The Lord's victory had been built on the shoulders of giants from the first phase of West Indies cricket – the likes of George Challenor, Learie Constantine and George Headley. But it was also a triumph on behalf of the new generation of West Indians who had begun to settle in the UK since the arrival of the first 500 emigrants by boat on the *Empire Windrush* in 1948. 'In those days black people were more or less given a hard time', Walcott told the BBC many years later.[21] 'After that Test they said how proud they felt to go into work or to school … having beaten England.'[22]

For his own part Walcott experienced no outright racial prejudice on the tour, although he reported that 'in the smaller places people tended to stare at us'[23] and that on one occasion in Nottingham, which he thought comical, an old lady rubbed his hand to see if the colour would come off. The regular supportive presence of a coterie of UK-based West Indian students helped the team to feel more at home, and he thoroughly enjoyed the trip, establishing his reputation as a good man to have on tour.

Apart from an over-preponderance of official functions, with their demands for boring small talk, just about the only thing that Walcott became tired of was the monotonous hotel food of austerity Britain, with its beef, boiled potatoes and boiled cabbage. As the players' weekly allowance did not stretch to regular eating out, he joined a delegation to the tour manager, the Bajan former cricketer Jack Kidney, to ask for a solution. The result was an extra fee whenever the team was in London that gave the squad license to eat at a Chinese restaurant in Soho run by the boxing celebrity Freddy Mills, where the fare was much more to their liking.

The Victory Test at Lord's drew the West Indies level at 1–1 for the series, and with comfortable wins at Trent Bridge and the Oval in the third and fourth Tests – the latter by an innings – a turnaround was completed. The West Indies were firmly established, for the first time, among the great cricketing powers. Ram and Val notwithstanding, the three Ws, as widely predicted, had been highly influential in the outcome. Worrell averaged 89 in the Tests, with Weekes on 56 and Walcott 45. Across the tour they were also the biggest run-getters, Weekes with 1,972 at 85, Walcott with 1,445 at 57 and Worrell with 1,236 at 61.

While Walcott's 168 not out was his only major score in the Tests, he compiled seven centuries in all matches, and his overall contribution was of immense value, especially when his wicketkeeping was taken into account. After hitting his century at Lord's, he returned immediately to the field as England blocked out 191 overs before finally succumbing. In the second innings of the first Test at Old Trafford he even temporarily took off his keeping pads so that he could open the bowling, delivering four valuable overs for just 12 runs in the absence of Hophnie Johnson, who had been forced off with an injury. Walcott's final act of a highly successful tour was an exhilarating knock of 121 against H. D. G. Leveson Gower's XI at the Scarborough Festival, which included a stand of exactly 100 with Ramadhin, who contributed just 4 to the partnership.

Now a fully established – indeed core – member of the West Indies side, Walcott viewed the 1950 tour not just as a triumphant team undertaking but an invaluable personal success. Honing his batting skills for the first time in England, on all types of pitches, made him a more solid player who was adaptable to a variety of conditions, without taking away his great attacking gifts.

It also opened up fresh horizons, for on the tour he was approached to play as the professional for Enfield cricket club in the Lancashire League for the following summer in 1951. Walcott's commission-only insurance job back home in Barbados, while handily flexible, was unlikely ever to generate as much as a league cricket contract, and a season in Lancashire would also aid his game. After discussing the pros and cons with Worrell and Weekes, who had already been playing in the English leagues (for Radcliffe and Bacup respectively), he signed the deal.

With that financial good news in his back pocket, the arrival back in the Caribbean with the other players was doubly joyous. 'All Barbados turned out, so it seemed, to welcome us back', Walcott said. 'The scene as we came in was almost unbelievable. Crowds were swarming in every imaginable place, including the rigging of the several schooners in the harbour. All around, mingling with the enchanting sound of the steel bands, were people singing and cheering. It was a wonderful reception which made the trip even more worthwhile for us than it had seemed before.'[24]

Waiting at the harbour was Muriel Ashby, Walcott's girlfriend of the past two years. She was a year or so his junior, and they had started dating when they met at her uncle's chemist shop in Bridgetown, meeting regularly thereafter with Muriel's sister, Barbara, as a chaperone. Muriel, too, was from the black middle classes, though a notch up from Walcott's perch. Her father, Vere Ashby, had inherited the Plumgrove sugar estate near Oistins, about ten miles outside Bridgetown, where she had grown up in a large stone 'great house' built in the Palladian style, with cooks, cleaners and maids.

The Ashby family, according to Muriel's niece, Andrea Stuart, 'valued conventionality and a conspicuous respectability',[25] looking to British social norms for their outlook, with Vere Ashby 'an avuncular patriarch' and Muriel's mother (also a Muriel) 'a suitably submissive matriarch'.[26] Regular church attendance was mandatory, 'and like every affluent home they had antimacassars on the furniture and a piano in the lounge'.[27] Despite the servants and general air of prosperity, however, Plumgrove was a relatively small plantation, and money worries were often to the fore.

Walcott proposed to Muriel on his return from England, and they were married four months later on

31 January 1951, she aged 23 and he 25. Afterwards Walcott put his mind to selling insurance, scored heavily for Barbados in two matches against Trinidad in February 1951 – including a double century in the second – and began to make preparations for his season with Enfield. Travelling to England in April with Muriel, they were accompanied by Weekes and his own new bride, Joan, for an English summer of new experiences in the Lancashire League.

Enfield cricket club, situated in the small Lancashire town of Clayton-le-Moors on the edge of Accrington, had arranged for Walcott and Muriel to live in 'digs' with a local widow, whom they knew simply as 'Auntie Belle'. She was able to help them acclimatise to their new surroundings, although they found it difficult initially to get used to the cool, wet weather. For Walcott there was nets practice four nights a week and a league game every Saturday in front of a couple of thousand spectators, after which, for both of them, there was dancing or the cinema. On Sundays there were charity or friendly matches across the north of England that provided light relief from the pressure of league fixtures, often for a side of West Indians who were playing in the northern leagues. During one such event in May 1951, appearing for a West Indies XI against Barnoldswick in front of more than 4,000 spectators, Walcott hit a six into a euphonium that had been left on the boundary edge by a member of the Barnoldswick brass band, putting the instrument out of action.

The down-to-earth Lancashire locals took a shine to the exotic, newly married couple, and with a number of other West Indian cricketers nearby to remind them of home, Walcott and Muriel settled in well – even if in such a small community they existed in something of a goldfish bowl. 'There was no telephone in the house and every time we had to make a call we would walk to the kiosk at the end of the road', said Walcott.[28] 'The locals would say, "The pro has used the phone this morning" or "the pro was at the bank".'[29] Worrell, who played league cricket for Radcliffe, would often have open house for West Indian friends, including Walcott and Weekes; the players were better able to let their hair down behind closed doors with old acquaintances, as it was important not be seen out carousing before matches. Worrell was a big drinker in his Radcliffe days, but Walcott was never one for more than a couple of glasses.

Enfield had not won the league since 1909 and had no real prospect of doing so even with Walcott's exciting arrival, as they had finished rock-bottom the previous year. But he had an excellent season opening the batting, scoring 1,136 runs in 23 innings at an average of 71 while also taking 53 wickets with his tricky fast-medium, in-swinging off-cutters at 19.5. Aside from his contractual income, which would have been around £700 for the season, there were cash collections around the boundary whenever he clocked up a half century (11 times), a century (twice) or a five-wicket haul (3 times). Occasionally up to £20 would be inside the bag; he used the proceeds to finance trips with Muriel to Blackpool and Morecambe, travelling across in a Hillman Minx car that he had bought with his new-found wealth. At the season's end in September 1951, he gladly accepted an offer to come back the next year, and indeed played for a further three English summers at Enfield.

Given that the West Indies tour of Australia was beginning in November 1951, Walcott had neither the time nor the money to return to Barbados at the end of his first league campaign. Instead, Muriel, now pregnant with their first child, Michael, returned home on her own while her husband set sail for Perth on board SS *Strathmore* with six other West Indies players who had been playing in England as professionals in the leagues, including Weekes, Worrell and Ramadhin. Despite the sadness of his parting with Muriel, Walcott settled down into an enjoyable, self-regulated trip with net practice, table tennis, swimming and quoits on deck, and dancing down below in the evening. In advance of their departure, the small party had agreed to cut out the socialising once they got to Bombay, and from then onwards a strict training regime was followed until arrival in the port of Fremantle.

Despite that happy beginning, the nature of the 1951–52 Australian tour was in marked contrast to the triumphant visit to England of the previous year. The

five-game series had been billed as the world championship of cricket, but the West Indies did not stand
up to scrutiny, losing 4–1. The supportive internal
atmosphere of 1950 seemed to dissolve as internecine
divisions arose, and Walcott had a personally testing
time, with injury severely hampering his ability to
contribute to the team effort.

His main difficulty was his back, which began to
give him considerable pain during the very first match
of the tour, a friendly up-country encounter in New
South Wales in which he had landed badly on his
spine when taking a diving catch behind the stumps.
A few days later, in the first proper tour match against
Queensland, he added insult to injury by top-edging
a ball into his face while batting, breaking his nose.
Battered and bruised, he nonetheless took to the field
in the first Test at Brisbane, where he was out first
ball to the fearsome pace of Ray Lindwall – the only
duck he ever suffered in Test cricket. Walcott's batting
held up relatively well in the second Test in Sydney,
where he hit a determined first innings 60, but by
then his back had become so troublesome that he was
forced to miss the next two Tests. Specialists initially
diagnosed a slipped disc, but thanks to some highly
effective treatment from a local osteopath he was able
to reappear for the final Test in Sydney with the series
already lost. He did not, however, keep wicket in that
match, and never donned the gloves in a Test from that
point onwards.

**Figure 2.2** West Indies tour of England. PA Images/Alamy Stock Photo.

Walcott identified several reasons for the West Indies' failure in Australia, chief among them the simple fact that the team did not play to its full ability. But he also felt the schedule had been poorly organised, with only one serious match before the first Test to get the players accustomed to Australian conditions, and was critical of captain Goddard's decision-making and tactics. During the 1950 tour to England the skipper had encouraged input from his established players, some of whom – Walcott among them – had later felt that he took too much credit for the attendant triumphs.

According to Worrell, who had his own cooling-off in relations with Goddard, 'the annoyance was so great that [in] Australia the advice was withheld, leaving Goddard a captain without officers – and we drifted on the rocks'.[30] At the root of this may have been the undercurrent of dissatisfaction at being led by a white captain – although it has to be said that Stollmeyer, also white, was among those who seemed to withdraw cooperation.

The West Indies might, of course, have put up more of a fight if Walcott had been able to give of his all. 'Often I could only bend just far enough to hold a bat, and it was rare for me to have the freedom of movement to play smooth and effortless strokes', he said.[31] Although he actually topped the West Indies averages in first-class matches on tour, he could muster only 87 runs in his three Tests.

Nevertheless, some good came out of Walcott's tribulations, for he finally realised he could no longer satisfactorily combine wicketkeeping with frontline batting. Once he had made the decision to put away his gloves – after a valedictory match as wicketkeeper against South Australia in mid-December 1951 – his performances with the bat took on an even greater dimension. From now on he would generally field at slip, where his long reach was especially useful, and although he would occasionally be required to bowl his off-cutters, the dual responsibility of batting and keeping no longer tested his body or occupied his mind.

In some ways Walcott had never looked a convincing figure in wicketkeeping gear – he was too tall and burly, rather like an oversized jockey on a horse – but the appearance belied reality. 'At first sight one would be sceptical about his ability to keep wicket; such a huge man must be clumsy, one would feel', said Stollmeyer.[32] 'But see him stump on the leg side the misguided batsman who lifted his back foot, and you would have cause to alter your opinion. He improved immeasurably as time went by ... and graduated into the front rank of wicketkeepers.'[33]

Nimble and agile, he had been unchallenged in that position until his injuries in Australia, and was responsible for 57 catches and 11 stumpings in Test cricket. But his benefit to the West Indies as a batsman far outweighed his merits as a keeper, and it was the correct decision to call it a day. Over the 15 Tests in which he had kept wicket he averaged a very respectable 40 with the bat. Afterwards that figure went up to 66, the mark of a true great. In the two Tests against New Zealand that immediately followed the Australian tour, Walcott batted with renewed freedom, posting a century in the second of them in Auckland in February 1952. He was about to enter the most prolific phase of his career.

# India, Enfield and the Hutton tour

With the New Zealand leg of the five-month Australasian tour completed at the end of February 1952, Walcott made his way back to the UK in time for the start of a new league season in Lancashire with Enfield. There was no opportunity to be present at the birth of son Michael in Barbados in late March, and indeed he was not to get a first sight of him for another half year.

At Enfield, Walcott had another impressive season, helping the club to seventh position in the league – one better than during his first year – and scoring 955 runs in 20 innings at an average of 79.6, with 44 wickets at 16.1. By now the club had arranged for him to live with Vera, older sister of the future Lancashire player Jack Simmons, and her husband, Tommy, in their home close to the Enfield ground.

Walcott soon became part of the lively Simmons household, and took the young Jack under his wing, providing him with free private coaching, taking him on many of his trips as he played friendly matches on a Sunday, and sometimes treating his parents to a meal at the Lobster Pot restaurant in Blackpool. 'Clyde also liked my mother's cooking and he would often take some of his meals at our place', recalls Simmons.[1] 'He would walk the half mile or so from the ground to our house, and he was so popular that along the way people would come out of doors to stop him for a chat. He was very easy-going and would speak to everybody on the way down, even though he wouldn't really know half of them. He was a super player and an absolutely super person with it.'[2]

In late September of 1952 Walcott returned to Barbados. United at last with his wife and son, he enjoyed three months of relative inactivity on the island before the arrival in January 1953 of the Indians for their five-Test tour of the Caribbean, the first in which he was paid by the West Indies on a wholly professional basis.

Again the matches against India were hard to bring to a resolution. The West Indies won the series 1–0, but with four of the Tests drawn, and Walcott was frustrated by the visitors' slow play and conservative tactics. During the second Test at Bridgetown he was given out LBW by his uncle, Harold Walcott, two runs short of what would have been his first Test century in the Caribbean. Fortunately he only had to wait two more games to reach that milestone, with 125 in

British Guiana in the fourth Test. In the fifth match in Jamaica he followed up with 118 in the first innings, in which all three Ws scored spectacularly – Worrell joining the party with 237 and Weekes with 109. Across the five Tests Walcott gathered 457 runs at an average of 76.2, another hugely successful effort and vindication of his decision to ditch the keeping gloves.

At the end of the series he joined the Indians on a boat to the UK, arriving in readiness for a third season at Enfield. His fine form continued there, to the extent that near the end of June 1953 he had a scarcely believable batting average of 635, although by the season's end it had settled down to 101.5. Now bowling off-breaks in the league, he also had his best season with the ball, taking 52 wickets at 13.6 apiece across a campaign in which his team finished fifth. There was a match for a Commonwealth XI against an England XI in Kingston-upon-Thames in September 1953 before he was home again with Muriel shortly afterwards, ready for what turned out to be a tumultuous five-Test home series against England, who were captained for the first time by a professional, Len Hutton.

That 1953–54 series was Walcott's best yet – he scored 698 runs in the Tests at an average of 87.25, with three centuries and his highest ever Test innings of 220, which came at Bridgetown in the second match. The England bowler Brian Statham marked Walcott's 220 down as comfortably the best innings that was ever played against him, while for Michael Manley it 'represented the final ascent by Walcott to the pinnacle which he subsequently occupied in the hierarchy of West Indian batting'.[3] He was now challenging Hutton strongly for the title of the world's best batsman.

Again Weekes, Worrell and Walcott proved to be the key batting axis throughout the series, scoring 206, 167 and 124 respectively in the same innings in the fourth Test on the newly laid turf pitch in Trinidad – 'a large rum punch followed by champagne and a cocktail'[4] as Ernest Eytle put it – as the West Indies reached 681. England had a strong side featuring Trevor Bailey, Peter May, Denis Compton, Tom Graveney, Brian Statham, Tony Lock and Jim Laker, as well as 'fiery' Fred Trueman. The contest went down to the wire, with England winning the last Test in Jamaica to draw the series 2–2.

It was, however, a horrible series in many ways, ruined, in Walcott's view, by controversy and acrimony. The British Caribbean was in a state of dangerous flux when Hutton's men arrived. Tortuously slow moves towards independence were leading to frustration, while unrest and agitation for majority rule were gathering apace. Woefully briefed before they went out, the touring side had no real conception of what they were walking into, leaving them badly prepared to negotiate the minefield over which they trod.

More concerned with in-house agendas than the political ramifications of their presence at a time of

**Figure 3.1** West Indies tour of England. PA Images/Alamy Stock Photo.

anti-colonialist agitation, England's players could hardly have misread the runes more spectacularly. Over the five Test matches of the tour they drew widespread criticism in the West Indies for overly aggressive fast bowling, foul language on the field, gamesmanship, deliberate slow play and unseemly dissension over umpiring decisions, including some of those made by Walcott's Uncle Harold.

There were also allegations of racial insults, an unfortunate decision by the 'dour and ruthless'[5] Hutton to avoid off-field fraternisation with the opposition players, and a series of perceived snubs that culminated in the skipper being accused of ignoring the presence of Alexander Bustamante, nationalist chief minister of Jamaica, during the final Test in Kingston.

In addition, the series was marked by serious crowd trouble in British Guiana, suspected pitch tampering in Trinidad, and the no-balling of England's Tony Lock for throwing. Given the multitude of flashpoints, Walcott felt it was a stormier encounter even than the controversial bodyline series of the 1930s. The England side, he said, were 'the most unpopular ever to tour the Caribbean',[6] making little or no effort to engage either with the West Indies team or the populace.

While Walcott never alluded directly to any racial slights delivered by the opposition, he did say that 'some of the language directed against our players was appalling',[7] and later comments made by Hutton on his return to England only served to reinforce the idea that racial tensions underlay some of the difficulties encountered in the series. In his book *Just My Story*, chronicling the tour, Hutton complained about 'the gradual exclusion of white folk'[8] from West Indies cricket, arguing that it was detrimental for the game – a statement that was met with incredulity by Walcott. 'When the 1950 West Indian side went to England, eight of the 16 players were white,' Walcott said.[9]

> By the time of the 1953–54 tour that total had been whittled down to a handful. The team was picked on merit and the change was inevitable. For the England captain to claim whites were being excluded implied discrimination against whites was taking place, and that was just not so. My feelings at the time were, 'Does he think that coloured people, on grounds of education or intelligence, are incapable of maintaining the traditions and standards of the game?'[10]

Aside from the racial angle, Walcott was perhaps more surprised at the lack of sportsmanship displayed by the England team, arguing that if the boot had been on the other foot, the whole West Indies touring side would probably have been sent home in disgrace. 'The laws clearly state that the captain is responsible for ensuring that play is conducted within the spirit of the game, and I am afraid Len Hutton had much to answer for on that tour', he said.[11] 'He was a fine tactician but a captain needs more than that to succeed. He must be a good disciplinarian and a leader of men.'[12]

# Clyde Walcott

Walcott's disappointment at the lack of sportsmanship was particularly acute given that his upbringing and education in Barbados had been based so substantially around the idea of British fair play. Although he was under no illusions about the frailties of man, he still revered the English as the progenitors of the game – and the supposed upholders of its traditional values. During the 1953–54 series it appeared to Walcott that he and his fellow teammates were far more committed to those principles than their opponents. Certainly Walcott himself was renowned for his own impeccable behaviour, and he had a marked distaste for seeing anyone step away from the standards that he so rigidly conformed to.

That said, Walcott had some sympathy for individual England players on some fronts: the row over Hutton's supposed snubbing of Bustamante was a political concoction, he thought, and although he was annoyed at the behaviour of Fred Trueman throughout the series, he recognised that the spirited young bowler, who had hardly set foot out of Yorkshire up to that point, ought to have received better guidance and support. He picked out Willie Watson, Peter May, Godfrey Evans and Jim Laker as pleasurable companions on and off the field, and later struck up a happy relationship with Trueman.

The West Indies needed only a draw in the final Test to win the series, but Walcott's fighting 116 in a second innings total of 346 was not enough to rescue

the cause. It was a series the West Indies should probably have won, given their home advantage and the
strength of their batting. 'As so often happens when a
side thinks it has a powerful batting line-up, we failed
dismally', he said.[13]

After the completion of the England tour in early
April 1954, Walcott was off again to Enfield for what
would turn out to be a valedictory Lancashire League
season.[14] During the series against England he had been
approached to move in an entirely new direction as a
cricket organiser on the vast sugar estates of British
Guiana, a job that would base him in that country for
the next 16 years.

# 4

# To British Guiana

Walcott's sojourn in British Guiana lasted from 1954 to 1970 and was, by his own account, one of the most satisfying periods of his life. During those years he served first as cricket organiser and then as social welfare organiser for the British Guiana Sugar Producers' Association, an umbrella body of the various large sugar estates that dominated the territory. The work he contributed to in those two roles had a marked effect on the social and economic wellbeing of the country.

Once Walcott's season with Enfield had been completed, he travelled to British Guiana from England in the autumn of 1954, breaking the trip for two weeks to tie up loose ends in Barbados before crossing the 450 miles to his new home on the South American mainland with Muriel on 15 October. 'Cricket in the colony has been at a very low ebb in recent years, and it is hoped that Walcott's presence will stimulate youngsters throughout the colony so that greater enthusiasm and ultimate improvement will be seen',[1] said the local *Daily Argosy* newspaper two days later.

Like the rest of the British West Indies at that stage, British Guiana was a colony, although with some emerging semblance of local governance and a burgeoning movement in favour of self-rule. With an area comparable to the British Isles (83,000 square miles) but a population of less than 500,000, most of the country was uninhabited tropical rainforest, with the vast majority of the population confined either to the capital, Georgetown, with its preponderance of pretty wooden buildings, or to the flat, low-lying areas near the Atlantic coast, where the sugar plantations were sited on fertile land that had often been reclaimed from the sea.

Unlike Walcott's home island of Barbados, where the vast majority of people were of African heritage, British Guiana had a large population of Indian descent whose forbears had been invited to the country between 1838 and 1917 to work as indentured labourers on the sugar plantations after the abolition of slavery. Only around a third had ever returned home, and so by the 1890s a sizeable population of Indian origin had been established. By the time Walcott arrived in the country, they made up roughly 40 per cent of the population, with the remainder largely of African descent.

Although since colonisation British Guiana had generated income through various activities, including

**Figure 4.1** Seymour cartoon in the *Guiana Sunday Graphic*, 17 October 1954.

mining, the sugar plantations remained the dominant feature of life. Generating significant wealth for various individuals and companies for many years, they had also created, as the Guyanese literary scholar Gordon Rohlehr characterised it, 'a natural by-product of degraded and tension-ridden human relationships',[2] based on a feudal system with white estate managers and owners at the top and the mainly Indian workforce at the bottom.

Conditions for workers were often little better than during the days of slavery, with families jammed together in airless, windowless 'logies' – living accommodation that had been used for slaves before abolition. Wages were low, there was little provision for sanitation or education, and there was widespread illiteracy and poverty. Periodic uprisings, strikes and rebellions were often put down with force.

From the 1890s onwards a few sugar planters began to try to ward off such unrest by introducing improvements, such as the provision of plots of land for workers on which they could grow rice and graze cattle in their spare time. They also began to promote the game of cricket as 'a force for long term stability and concord on the estates',[3] particularly among the young.

'Indian boys born in the colony took to cricket with as much enthusiasm as their parents embraced rice and cattle farming', said the Guyanese historian Clem Seecharan: 'The impact of the game on the community as a whole was profound. On every plantation in every village, on patches of ground between logies on the estates, and on reefs in the cattle pasture, these boys, whether of brahmin or charmar origin, Hindu or Muslim, played cricket with unbridled enthusiasm.'[4] Gradually cricket became, just as it had among the African people of British Guiana and in the wider Caribbean, a way for those at the lower end of the social scale to assert the worth and identity that were denied them in other spheres.

General social and economic progress on the plantations was, however, slow. It was only after the Second World War, prompted by strikes and further violent uprisings, the rise of the Marxist politician Cheddi Jagan, and the conclusions of the 1949 Venn Commission, which called for a programme of social improvements across the sugar estates, that wider-reaching social reforms began to be instituted in the early 1950s.

Chief protagonist in these sugar industry changes was the progressive figure of Jock Campbell, an Englishman with Fabian socialist sympathies who was chairman, from the early 1950s to the late 1960s, of the London-based company Booker, the pre-eminent sugar firm in British Guiana. Campbell, who was also head of the Sugar Producers' Association (SPA), had been influenced by the sweeping changes introduced in Britain by the Labour government of Clement Attlee after the Second World War, and had begun to increase the pace of reform on Booker plantations in British Guiana via the 'Jock Campbell Revolution', a thorough-going programme of social welfare that included the creation of community centres and cricket grounds on all estates.

Campbell was also a key figure in the negotiation of the Commonwealth Sugar Agreement of 1951, under which the UK government agreed to take set amounts of sugar from countries such as British Guiana at a guaranteed minimum price. As a quid pro quo, Booker and other sugar estate owners in British Guiana agreed to put money into a Sugar Industry Labour Welfare Fund, which soon had millions of Guyanese dollars available for social reforms.

It was Campbell who came up with the inspired notion of appointing a cricket organiser, and it was he who made the formal approach to Walcott in February 1954, while Walcott was playing in Georgetown for the West Indies in the third Test of the home series against England.

Although it took several weeks for Walcott to mull the offer over, he had certainly accepted the job by springtime, for British papers reported news of his appointment in late April of that year, stating that he would go to British Guiana 'as soon as he has completed a contract with the Enfield club of the Lancashire League'.[5] In fact he had previously made a gentleman's agreement to play for two more seasons at Enfield, but when the club heard of his new plans they agreed not to stand in his way. He recommended Nyron Asgarali, of Trinidad, to replace him, and Asgarali played for Enfield for two seasons after Walcott's departure, in 1955 and 1956.

Once Walcott had arrived in British Guiana, he, Muriel and Michael initially lived in temporary accommodation on the Lusignan sugar estate, about ten miles east of Georgetown, before moving six months later to a rent-free family home in Regent Street, Georgetown, a comfortable three-bedroomed colonial-style house close to Bourda cricket ground, where he began to play for Georgetown Cricket Club and where he also joined the local Mount Olive masonic lodge. From his base in the capital he would travel by car to the sugar plantations on an almost daily basis, staying overnight in estate guest houses when required.

Walcott's role as cricket organiser was to build and organise community and cricket facilities under the auspices of the SPA. Tasked with travelling around the country to improve the standard of competitive cricket, he also had a brief to foster coaching across the estates and to spot new talent that could be nurtured at regional and national level.

Initially, as Walcott conceded, there was 'a certain degree of suspicion'[6] among the Guyanese population about the parachuting-in of a Barbadian, not just due to local hubris but because Walcott had spent many

**Figure 4.2** Estate manager houses at Lusignan sugar estate, where Walcott lived for his first six months in British Guiana. Author photo.

years previously as an enemy combatant playing for Barbados in opposition to British Guiana.

Two months into his job, in December 1954, the matter came to a head during the build-up to British Guiana's forthcoming trip to Barbados for a two-match series beginning in January 1955. Walcott was keen to show that, having emigrated to the country, his loyalties now lay with the British Guiana cricket team, and was determined to switch to play for his new territory. But qualification rules set by the West Indies Cricket Board of Control stipulated that he could only appear for a different team once he had lived in the country for at least a year. Given that Walcott desperately needed to play in top-level cricket as a warm-up for the imminent arrival of Australia for a Test series against the West Indies, there was much discussion as to whether he would, in the end, bite the bullet and play for Barbados.

It was, for Walcott, 'a most embarrassing position',[7] but fortunately one that was eventually resolved with special pleading to the West Indies Board in December 1954, when it agreed to a one-off waiver of its regulations to allow him to become a British Guiana player with immediate effect.

Although that circumstance allowed some of the suspicions about Walcott to lessen, unfortunately the trip to Barbados did much to raise them again. Playing under the captaincy of Bruce Pairaudeau in the first innings of the first match against Barbados,

Walcott tweaked his back while batting, continuing at the crease to make exactly 50 when he should really have retired hurt. Compounding the problem, he then decided to come out to bat in the second innings when Pairaudeau needed help in a sticky situation, making 17 in a futile effort to try to save the match. His time at the crease worsened the injury, and as a result he could not take part in the second match – fuelling speculation that he was reluctant to play against his old teammates. 'As I had gone to some trouble to obtain special permission to play, the rumours were ridiculous', he said later, 'but they were nevertheless worrying, as the confidence of local cricket followers would be necessary to me in my job'.[8]

In the final analysis, however, Walcott's concerns were unfounded, for within short order he had managed to establish himself, by sheer force of commitment and personality, as a trusted member of Guyanese society. In fact, Walcott's initial status as an outsider may actually have helped to smooth his acceptance, as he found himself helpfully disentangled from many of the social, racial and economic knots in which Guyanese society was tied. His standing in the colony had also benefited from his decision to move to the country in the first place, given that it had been experiencing violent political turbulence since 1953, when the British had suspended its nascent constitution and sent in troops to quell protests. Walcott reported that friends back home had advised him on several occasions to leave the country for his own safety, but he and Muriel were set on staying.

In British Guiana at large, Clyde and Muriel, who later became a librarian at the United States Information Service in Georgetown, became valued members of polite society. 'We used to meet them at sugar industry meetings and so on, but also on the cocktail party circuit and at small dinner parties with mutual friends',[9] says Ian McDonald, a senior sugar industry executive in British Guiana from the mid-1950s onwards.

> I remember them as being delightful people, very easy to get on with. Clyde certainly wasn't just interested in cricket, although what he was doing in British Guiana was very important to him – he was very well read and was willing and able to discuss all sorts of things, although he was careful not to stray into politics. It was quite clear that he and Muriel were very close, and they always came across as a very solid middle-class couple.[10]

McDonald recalls that while Walcott was always comfortable at any gathering, 'he was not a social animal as such',[11] and the Guyanese cricket commentator Reds Perreira, who lived near the Walcotts in the 1950s and 1960s, concurs. 'He wasn't a big socialiser', says Perreira.[12] 'If he was invited to a function then he would happily attend – and he would enjoy it, as he was good at mixing and talking. But he wasn't a party man, and he wouldn't be seen in bars or anything like that. He would take a drink or two and that would be it.'[13] Muriel, say both men, was a friendly, supportive and intelligent presence, always sporting a ready smile, unfailingly pleasant and a lover of jazz music. She also had a thorough understanding of cricket in all its aspects, and tolerated Walcott's cricketing absences with a minimum of fuss.

Walcott's brief as the SPA's cricket organiser theoretically spread across the whole of British Guiana, although in reality he was confined mainly to operating in the large, sweltering coastal areas to the east of Georgetown – in East Coast Demerara and Berbice – where sugar plantations could be found in profusion, all the way across to the border with Dutch Guiana (later Surinam). The huge, sparsely inhabited Amerindian interior was mainly rainforest or savannah, with few cricket grounds and no sugar plantations to speak of, while in the less remote, but generally overlooked, Essequibo region to the west of Georgetown, the sugar industry had become defunct by the mid-1930s. Walcott had no engagement with that county, and it remains an area of darkness a far as the documented history of Guyanese cricket is concerned.

A first survey of the situation showed that Walcott had a big job on his hands; in fact, 'by far the most challenging task I had [ever] undertaken'.[14] Although there were plans for new facilities on most estates, in general those he inherited were in a poor state,

with most of the cricket grounds having barely ser-
viceable, rough dirt pitches. In addition, very few, if
any, of the cricketers on the estates had ever been
properly coached.

'When I arrived and saw the facilities I realized what
a mammoth task I faced to develop the game in the
plantations', he said; 'I had to organise the clubs and
the competitions and advise on improving facilities,
persuading the [estate] owners to put down concrete
pitches in the outlying areas that would survive the
harsh climate.'[15]

Aged only 28 when appointed, Walcott had plenty
of physical and intellectual energy to offer the job, and
he put it to good use in his new environment. After an
exhaustive inspection tour of all the sugar plantations
in the country, he began to oversee the building of new
grounds on some estates and to supervise improvements
on others – while also embarking on a rationalisation
programme to amalgamate the profusion of local teams.
In future, each estate would have just one club, rather
than a ragbag of smaller, rival outfits.

Helped by the enthusiasm of the cricket-mad,
mainly Indian population of the estates, Walcott made
excellent progress in a relatively short time. Once
some of the physical improvements had been set in
motion, he was able to turn his attention more fully
to the coaching and talent-spotting side of the job.
By the end of 1954 he had already performed some
general coaching and pastoral duties at the Leonora

and Uitvlugt estates on West Coast Demerara, followed by a visit to Plantation Skeldon on the Upper Corentyne, where he spoke to a packed meeting of young cricketers about various aspects of batting, bowling and fielding. At that gathering, and on subsequent coaching assignments, Walcott also showed a short film in which he demonstrated some of the technical skills he was hoping to see widely adopted throughout the territory. He also stressed that he was on the lookout for hidden talent, and was careful to ask around for news of any locally talented players while on his tours of the estates.

In this task he was greatly helped by his former West Indies teammate Robert Christiani, a Guyanese cricketer who had been working as personnel manager on the Port Mourant estate since before Walcott's arrival. Christiani already knew much about who was worth watching in the plantation sides, but Walcott brought a new vigour and determination to the task, as well as a special talent for engaging with young players once they had been spotted. What he discovered was that the sugar belt was a hotbed of talented, if raw, cricketers, and that with some pastoral care he could bring those players on to the next level.

Much of the gold that Walcott found was contained in a rich seam at the Port Mourant estate in Berbice, where it transpired that four cricketers of huge promise – Rohan Kanhai, Basil Butcher, Joe Solomon and Ivan Madray – all lived. Walcott immediately latched onto their potential, and while he acknowledged the help of Christiani in bringing them to his initial attention – describing the older man's assistance as 'invaluable'[16] – there seems little doubt that much of the credit for making the most of their talent must go to the Barbadian.

Until Walcott's arrival, only two players from the sugar estates had been able to emerge to play cricket for British Guiana – the fast-medium bowler John Trim, from Port Mourant, who made his debut in 1944 and also played in four Tests for the West Indies from 1948 to 1952, and Sonny 'Sugar Boy' Baijnauth, from Plantation Albion, who first appeared for British Guiana in 1947. Otherwise, the remote lands of Berbice had been out of sight and out of mind for the 'the czars of Georgetown still marooned in class and colour prejudices'.[17]

As an outsider with no homegrown loyalties or prejudices, Walcott was determined to address that waste of talent. He could discover no valid reason why 'coolies' from the sugar estates should not form the backbone of future British Guiana sides, and from the start, as Seecharan has observed, 'he made rural players, the backwoodsmen, feel as if they mattered'.[18]

Walcott's inclusive style was an immediate attraction for a set of young Port Mourant players who had previously felt ignored by the cricketing authorities and, as small boys, had sometimes even been shooed away from the Port Mourant ground by older players. The leg-break bowler Ivan Madray remembered first meeting Walcott in late 1954, when the new cricket organiser came to Port Mourant as part of an early tour of Berbice sugar estates. Making his way to Roopmahal's cinema, Walcott asked the proprietor to get a message to Madray, Kanhai and Butcher to meet him there later. When they eventually turned up, he invited them all to a bazaar that was taking place at the local Anglican school that evening. 'I said "skipper, I can't go, I don't have money"', said Madray.

> But he replied: 'don't worry, come along.' He gave me three dollars to buy a pair of yachting shoes [before we went there] and he also gave Rohan and Butch money, too. He took us in his car that evening to the bazaar, paid for us to go in, spoke with us for a while and then left us to enjoy ourselves. The next thing we knew was that we were playing the trials in preparation for the Australian tour of British Guiana.[19]

Walcott, Madray said, had 'made up his mind, over the heads of the Georgetown bigots, to go out and find us'.[20]

The impact of Walcott's unexpected interest in Kanhai, Madray, Solomon and Butcher was life-changing for each of them. When Kanhai played in his debut first-class match in February 1955 at the age of 19, he had not even seen a first-class match, let alone played in one, and, as Seecharan observed, 'had probably never eaten with knife and fork'.[21] With Walcott a reassuring presence in the background, however, he was able to get a half century in his next match against the touring Australians. After impressive centuries for British Guiana against Jamaica and Barbados in 1956, Kanhai's West Indies debut came on the 1957 tour of England and he went on to win 79 Test caps.

Though Madray's wider career never quite took off – he played four times for British Guiana but just twice for the West Indies – Butcher (who was of African-Amerindian descent) played 44 Test matches from 1958 to 1969; and Solomon, picked up slightly later by Walcott, made his British Guiana debut in 1956, with selection in 27 Tests for the West Indies from 1958 to 1965.

The Port Mourant triumvirate of Kanhai, Solomon and Butcher eventually put themselves at the heart of the Frank Worrell-led West Indies team of the early 1960s that captivated the Commonwealth with the vibrancy of its play. But there were others, too, whose lot was improved by Walcott, even if their careers did not quite stretch to playing for the West Indies. The batsman Sonny Moonsammy, from Skeldon estate, the medium-pace bowler Saranga Baichu (Springlands) and the batsman Leslie Amsterdam (Blairmont) all surged through Walcott's programme to play for British Guiana in the 1958–59 season – and beyond. Later he helped to nurture the first-class careers of Charran Bissoon, Basil Mohabir, Randolph Ramnarace and Isaac Surienarine, all of whom were from the sugar lands.

'For the first time it became virtually impossible for a young player of real promise to go unnoticed', said Butcher. 'Quite possibly neither Rohan Kanhai, Joe Solomon nor I would have reached Test cricket under the old system.'[22] More generally, a whole generation of less talented players were able to improve and enjoy their cricket thanks to the changes that Walcott and the SPA introduced.

The new arrangements constructed by Walcott involved not just new facilities and coaching networks, but a reinvigorated tournament structure that ratcheted up the competitive cricketing atmosphere in the colony. Annual representative matches for the Jones Cup, between the three counties in British Guiana – Demerara, Essequibo and Berbice – had been set up the year before Walcott's appointment, but when Berbice, with a majority of players drawn from the sugar estates, won the trophy in its first two years, cricketing interest in that previously overlooked county was greatly enhanced. 'The impact on the public in Berbice was marvellous', says Reds Perreira.[23] 'All of a sudden attendances were up to 3,000 or 4,000 people for some matches. Walcott opened up cricket in rural Guyana.'[24]

Shortly after his arrival, Walcott was also instrumental in the creation of the Campbell Cup (named after Jock), which was competed for by four elite sugar plantation teams from six districts, drawing on the best players only. Allied to the Davson Cup, a longer established and more drawn-out competition that was also played on a plantation basis, as well as the pre-existing Rohlehr Cup and Flood Cup competitions, players in the colony now had a full range of keenly contested trophies to compete for – although the Davson and Rohlehr Cups were confined to the county of Berbice and the Flood Cup was contested for by Indians only, in the three counties of Essequibo, Demerara and Berbice.

At the same time as generating a greater amount of cricket in order to raise standards, Walcott tried to raise the general level of the game in other ways, including by introducing training schemes for umpires in the hope that this would improve general discipline. He also harnessed the expertise of the Trinidadian-born Olympic sprinter McDonald Bailey, who worked for the SPA as a general sports organiser, to develop programmes to improve the athleticism of the cricketers under his charge.

All of this soon fed into a higher level of attainment in local cricket. At the point of Walcott's arrival, British Guiana had failed to win a match against Trinidad, Barbados or Jamaica since 1951, and were patently the poorest of the main West Indian cricketing colonies. However, in 1956, by which time Walcott was captain and selector, they were able to essay a significant turnaround by winning the unofficial quadrangular regional championship.

Mustering a strong side that made full use of Kanhai, Butcher, Solomon, Madray and Baijnauth, plus another recent discovery from outside the sugar estates, the 22-year-old spin bowler Lance Gibbs, Walcott's young side showed guts to make it through to the final against Barbados in Georgetown, where they racked up 581 all out in a marathon first innings. Two days were lost to rain on what turned out to be a six-day match, and when Barbados followed on after being dismissed for 211, they finished at 67 for 4 on the final day – a draw, but with British Guiana winning the tournament by virtue of a superior first innings total.

It was a fine performance, grittily led by a quietly determined Walcott, and a landmark victory that put the colony back on the cricketing map, giving notice to the West Indies selectors that a host of Guyanese players might now be worthy of their consideration. It was no coincidence that Kanhai made his debut for the West Indies in 1957, and Butcher, Madray and Solomon appeared soon afterwards in 1958–59.

That quadrangular victory, which did much to lift the spirits of the local populace, was based not just on a harnessing of fresh talent but on Walcott's unstinting insistence on discipline. Having observed that too many players appeared satisfied with brisk 40s or 50s, he would tell the batsman in his strong Bajan accent: 'you got to bat on, and you got to bat long', a trademark phrase he became famous for delivering throughout the rest of his career. During speeches on sugar estates he also emphasised the importance of leadership, good manners, strength of character and attention to the psychological aspects of the game – a philosophy he stressed, and applied, many years later when, as manager of the West Indies, he worked with Clive Lloyd to turn the regional side into a world-beating unit.

In British Guiana Walcott could get across his points from a position of particular authority, for he had just been appointed vice-captain of the West Indies, had played monumentally well in the 1955 home series against Australia, and was one of the leading international players of his generation, commanding huge respect all round. But he also demonstrated powers of empathy, compassion and persuasion. Some of his charges – Kanhai and Madray in particular – were fiery individuals from harsh, underprivileged backgrounds who nursed wider resentments about their treatment at the hands of Guyanese society and needed careful handling. Walcott saw this, and was able to make a meaningful contribution to their personal as well as technical development, building their self-belief and self-worth. This he did with all the players he coached and mentored, from the top heights down to much lower levels of achievement. Though he was from a different racial and social milieu than most of the cricketers he dealt with, he seemed to understand the wider forces that buffeted them, and as a result became a positive force in many people's lives.

As a consequence, the level of loyalty that Walcott generated was often close to overwhelming. 'I could have walked to the end of the earth for Clyde Walcott', said Madray. 'He always brought out the best in me ... I never wanted to let him down. He was like a father, or a dear uncle.'[25] Many players felt they performed better when Walcott was by their side – and demonstrably worse when he was not. Madray, for instance, believed that when he made his debut for the West Indies in 1958, during a match against Pakistan in which Walcott was unable to play through injury, the absence of his mentor was one of the key reasons that he fluffed his lines.

'Walcott's technical and ethical standards were high, and he sought continually to inculcate a culture of discipline and respect for the traditions of the game', says Seecharan. 'But above all his was a towering presence that infused cricket in British Guiana with a sense of purpose and a resolve that had eluded it for most of its existence.'[26]

The first three years of Walcott's reign in British Guiana were pivotal in transforming the colony from a largely disregarded backwater to a mainstream source of talent for West Indies cricket. It was a dramatic turnaround, and an improvement that was built upon over the ensuing years. He led British Guiana to another regional tournament win in 1961, and continued to captain the side with success until 1964, making use of the fine core of players he had identified and nurtured. He also laid the ground for the emergence of other sugar estate cricketers who followed, including Roy Fredericks (from the Blairmont estate) and Alvin Kallicharran (Port Mourant), both of whom emerged in the mid-1960s and who, respectively, went on to play 59 and 66 Test for the West Indies. Clive Lloyd, though from Georgetown, also benefited from Walcott's wisdom, making his debut for British Guiana in 1964 and winning his first West Indies cap in 1966.

By that time almost everyone in British Guiana had been won over by Walcott's activities – including the old guard in the capital. 'To be fair to the Georgetown people, it seems to me they were quite happy, most of them anyway, to accept the blood transfusion', said Ian McDonald. 'I remember a high-up at Georgetown Cricket Club telling me that if Clyde was up in the [remote] Rupununi for a year, we would soon have the first Amerindian playing for the West Indies.'[27]

Was the success, though, primarily down to Walcott? Some, including C. L. R. James, seem to have thought as much. But it would be wrong to give full and absolute credit to the Barbadian. For one thing, praise must be due to the SPA, and in particular to Jock Campbell, for setting the ball rolling. Had Campbell selected someone other than Walcott to deliver the goods, then the outcomes may well have been less favourable. Yet Campbell chose well, and also made wise use of the money and influence at his disposal, laying solid foundations on which Walcott could build, especially at the heart of the revolution in Port Mourant, which proved to be an extraordinary breeding ground for cricketing talent.

Port Mourant, in the Corentyne District of Berbice, was at the epicentre of much of the good work that was carried out in British Guiana to improve living conditions on the sugar estates after the Second World War. Its relatively enlightened pre-war manger, J. C. Gibson, had built a framework by allowing its predominantly Indian workers to graze cattle, grow rice and build their own cottages on estate lands, and he also set up Port Mourant Sports Club in 1916 'to foster the playing of cricket'. Although situated in a relatively malaria-free zone, Port Mourant also benefited – as did the whole of British Guiana – from the pioneering work of the Italian tropical disease specialist George Giglioli, who in 1948, as medical officer for the SPA, was largely responsible through the use of DDT for eradicating the debilitating scourge of malaria across the land. The resultant improvement in health and outlook of the nation was transformative.

Once Campbell and the SPA began to implement other liberating improvements, including the provision of community centres, creches, cooking and literacy classes and canteens, Port Mourant flourished as a centre of energy, industry, flair and imagination – not least in cricket – and became an ideal petri dish into which Walcott could insert his ideas. What grew there was exceptional, but was also indicative of other less dramatic results on other estates.

So while Walcott's efforts appeared to produce results with incredible speed, in fact they were 'long in the making',[28] built on the work of others. The ground had been tilled, the seeds planted and the harvest swiftly reaped.

That said, it seems unlikely that many other people could have replicated Walcott's achievement, even given the same circumstances. There had been admired facilitators shortly before him – including the Port Mourant cricket club captain Johnny Teekasingh and, to a lesser extent, Trim and Christiani. Yet while their efforts had been appreciated by many young players, they proved powerless to harness the sugar estate talent to any effective degree, even with a supportive raft of social reforms taking place in the background. By contrast, Walcott had the authority, experience and emotional intelligence to take things forward.

Of course many of the playing resources were in place before the advent of Walcott. Kanhai, Butcher and Solomon were naturally gifted individuals who each required a minimum of technical instruction – 'my job was to guide them and advise them on how to make the best possible use of that talent', Walcott said.[29] But it was Walcott who helped those players to emerge into the light, who provided them with a platform to perform, fine-tuned their skills and engaged their talent in a way that turned them into top-class cricketers – in double quick time. It is entirely possible that none of the 'discoveries' from Port Mourant would have gone on to play representative or Test cricket were it not for the changes that he instituted, or the wise counsel that he offered.

Walcott's outsider status, though at first a concern, also proved to be important in delivering such impressive results. 'It was his perceived even-handedness, coupled with the fact that he was not a Guyanese and therefore above the partisan … political atmosphere of British Guiana from the mid-1950s, that made it possible for him to proffer critical judgment while earning the respect of those [he] criticised', says Seecharan. 'He was an almost unique example, in [a] highly politicised and racially charged colony, of an individual asking the right questions and moving efficaciously from diagnosis to resolution.'[30] It would certainly have been difficult for any Guyanese to break the stranglehold of the Georgetown elite in the way that Walcott did. But above all it was the supportive atmosphere that Walcott was able to generate – the positive charge he released into the air – that proved to be the catalyst for change. Almost overnight, he generated enthusiasm and hope.

In the process, and almost as a side-effect, Walcott's organisational achievements in British Guiana did a great deal to change the general outlook of the country's Indian population. By helping Kanhai to reach the pinnacle of the game in the early 1960s, Walcott brought huge pride and new self-confidence to a sector of society – not just in British Guiana, but in Trinidad, where the Indian population was also large – that had previously thought itself to be on the periphery of West Indian affairs. In a region where cricket has long been invested with inordinate significance, it is no exaggeration to say that Kanhai's achievements on the world stage, enabled and empowered by Walcott, did as much as anything to make the descendants of indentured labourers feel that they at last belonged to the Caribbean.

Walcott's period as cricket organiser lasted for around eight years, during which time his attention was inevitably drawn to wider social welfare issues at play in British Guiana, especially as independence was looming. Cricket was a crucial plank in the SPA's social reform programme, based as it was around the multipurpose sports and community centres it had been creating on sugar estates. But there were many other elements to the project.

As cricket organiser, Walcott had been one of the most senior members of a large SPA social welfare team that also included a women's welfare adviser, a medical adviser, a sanitation officer, an industrial relations officer, a sports organiser, a statistical officer and a social welfare organiser.

That last role, which effectively headed the SPA's entire social welfare programme, had been held for a number of years by a Yorkshireman, Ralph Scargall, who had previously been a youth worker in British Guiana and secretary of the YMCA in Georgetown. From an early juncture Walcott appears to have had an eye on taking over from Scargall should the opportunity ever arise – writing less than three years into his period in British Guiana that he was looking forward to 'the prospect of involving myself more deeply in social work in general'.[31] To that end he arranged to remain behind in London after the 1957 West Indies tour of England to undertake a tutorial course in social studies with the Industrial Welfare Society, which kept him in London until late December. The eight months he was away in 1957, with the agreement of the SPA, was the only significant period he was absent from British Guiana in all the time he was resident in the country, although he did take time off to play various home-series Test matches.

When, shortly after Walcott's return from England, Scargall announced that he would be taking early retirement due to ill health, the SPA began to prepare the ground for Walcott to take over his role. Most likely on Walcott's recommendation, his former protégé Joe Solomon was appointed as the SPA's new cricket organiser, allowing Walcott to move over into Scargall's former job while retaining an advisory role on the cricketing front.

For most of the 1960s, then, Walcott's focus was as much on the other aspects of the SPA's social welfare programmes as it was on cricket, although the two clearly went hand in hand. Having already achieved a great deal on the sporting front, he felt ready to continue Scargall's pioneering work in other areas, especially as by 1960, at the age of 34, he had played his last Test match and no longer had the distraction of international cricketing commitments.

At Campbell's behest, Scargall had been instrumental in the development of many improvements across the sugar estates, including the introduction of loans to help workers rent or buy new homes, the formation of community councils and tenants' associations, social clubs, creches and libraries on each estate, free milk for children, regular film shows and festivals, handicraft, adult education and home economics classes, as well as a host of other innovations, all of which it was now Walcott's job to oversee and, if possible, expand.

This he did in conjunction not only with colleagues on the SPA's general social welfare team, which he was responsible for managing, but with dedicated social welfare officers on each estate, whom he also oversaw. By 1963 he had proceeded to the point where community centres at each estate were run by the workers themselves, signalling a path forward on which workers might eventually take control of their own affairs.

At the heart of Walcott's next phase of work was a desire to foster a culture of self-help and spirit of independence on the estates, including through leadership training courses for young people (modules on which he was often a principal speaker) and for women. There were also scholarships for workers' children to study at home and abroad as part of a 'Guyanisation' programme that became so successful that when the sugar industry was eventually nationalised in 1976, it was already run almost exclusively by Guyanese.

The pace of change was quick during this early period of Walcott's control, as the sugar industry was keener than ever to respond to criticism of its supposedly malign influence by the two most popular rivals for post-independence power, Cheddi Jagan, an Indian from Port Mourant, and Forbes Burnham, an African from Georgetown. However, the substance of Walcott's work at this stage was also much disrupted by wider political and social discord, chiefly connected with the complex fight for independence and the attendant struggle for power between supporters of Jagan and Burnham. From the early 1960s onwards, as Jagan and Burnham fought each other for the highest office, the machinations of a prevaricating British government, allied to clandestine US interventions via the CIA, led to a powder keg situation in which Indians and Africans turned against each other in violent conflict on the streets. 'People who lived liked friends suddenly seemed to have lost their sense of reason and judgment', reported one of Walcott's social welfare officers, Baljit Ramdin, in 1963. 'There have been cases where people have said they will not [even] play cricket with people of any other race.'[32]

Far worse than non-participation in sports, many people were killed in confrontations or burnt out of their homes, and as the politics of bigotry took hold, it proved difficult to put back in its box. Among those who suffered from the racial violence was Basil Butcher, whose family was subject to an arson attempt at his home in Port Mourant, though fortunately with no loss of life.

In July 1963, in defiance of the political turbulence at large, Walcott organised a seminar for around 50 captains of cricket clubs. He spoke, along with the Test umpire Cecil Kippins and Kenny Wishart, secretary of the West Indies Cricket Board of Control, of the need to maintain racial unity and communal progress. By the following year, however, he was painfully aware that the use of estate community centres, sports grounds and other communal facilities had fallen dramatically, and that there was a danger that much of the SPA's good work could be lost forever. Communal violence, including an element of 'ethnic cleansing', had escalated alarmingly in the first half of 1964.

Thankfully, the protracted period of unrest began to die down when independence was finally granted in May 1966, though racial tensions remained for many years afterwards. Fortunately, too, Walcott was able to emerge personally unscathed from the situation, despite his position as a prominent African in the Indian-dominated landscape of the sugar estates.

As noted earlier, Walcott's relative detachment as a Barbadian incomer was a factor in his ability to stand above the fray, although his great diplomatic skills also came into play. 'As a foreigner, Walcott was better placed to negotiate the racial minefields of the Guyanese social and political landscape', says Seecharan.

> He was not readily located on either side of the racial chasm; neither was he inclined to casual venting of his emotions. Unlike many in [Guyanese] society, he was invariably circumspect, perhaps deliberately so. He was considered rational, non-partisan, and – of immense importance – one who was not intrinsically immersed in, and therefore could transcend, the racial predilection of this tortured colony at the end of Empire.[33]

Despite the violent alarms of the independence period, Walcott was later able to say that 'the vast majority supported me and my work',[34] and to report that the many friends he had made in British Guiana had stood by him when other relationships had been fracturing around him.

As it had been throughout his stay in the country, Walcott's personal existence outside cricket was still a generally happy one, and Muriel, too, enjoyed living in the country. Their second son, Ian, had been born in British Guiana not long after their arrival, and for many years they felt very settled. The pay was good, they lived in a desirable house in a pleasant part of Georgetown, and there was enough of a social life to fulfil their limited demands.

In 1968, however, Burnham, who had become the first prime minister of newly independent Guyana in 1966, had been returned to power in a fraudulent general election, ushering in a period of increasingly authoritarian and oppressive state control, underlined by racial tensions between Afro- and Indo-Guyanese. Standards of living began to fall dramatically, and many of Burnham's policies threatened much of what had been achieved through the SPA's programmes over the previous 20 years. A debilitating brain-drain began as thousands of Guyana's most talented individuals fled abroad in search of a better life. Walcott, too, concluded that it was time to go, opting for a return to Barbados in 1970. After 16 challenging, fruitful years in which he had created new hope in his adopted nation, his skills were lost to the country forever.

## 5

# Reaching a peak – and retirement

Walcott's work in British Guiana had become one of the most important aspects of his life from the mid-1950s onwards, but that did not mean his international cricket came to a halt. From 1955 to 1960 he played a further 16 Tests for the West Indies across four series, three of them at home and one away.

In the first of those encounters, at home to Australia in 1955, Walcott's batting reached its highest peak as he scored five centuries in five Tests – the first, and still only, batsman to do such a thing. In all probability he would have had six centuries, were it not for the misfortune of treading on his wicket as he was setting off for a run with his score on 73 in the third Test in Georgetown. He hit a century in both innings of a Test twice, and amassed the most runs ever scored by anyone in a Test series in the West Indies – 827, at an average of 82.70.

During that series he also became only the second West Indian to pass 3,000 Test runs (after Everton

Weekes) and at one point was able to join a small coterie of great players – including Don Bradman, George Headley and Herbert Sutcliffe – with a career Test average of more than 60, the culmination of a prodigious period in which he had knocked up ten centuries over the previous 12 Tests. For good measure he had also chipped in with four wickets in Tests during the series against Australia at 38 runs apiece, putting him third in the West Indies bowling averages.

Walcott's first century came in the first innings of the first Test, at Kingston, and was followed by 126 and 110 in the second Test on the newly laid turf wicket at Port of Spain, the first time he had scored centuries in both innings. Then he repeated the feat in the final Test back at Kingston with 155 and 110 – and yet the West Indies lost the match by an innings and 82 runs.

Walcott's run of scores in the five home Tests against Australia in 1955 read: 108, 39, 126, 110, 8, 73, 15, 83, 155 and 110 – an incredible sequence against bowlers of the class of Ray Lindwall, Keith Miller, Ian Johnson and Richie Benaud, and all the more remarkable because prior to the series he had injured his back again, playing for British Guiana against Barbados. Ordered to rest completely by his doctor, he had not been able to pick up a bat until ten days before the first Test.

By the end of the series Walcott was incontestably the best batsman in the world, standing out even above Worrell and Weekes as West Indies went down

3–0 in the series to a very strong Australia side. 'Over and over he stood like some Horatio at the bridge, his bat alone between West Indies shame and Australian onslaught',[1] said Manley, who compared Walcott's efforts to those of Headley between the wars.

Aside from the global acclaim they delivered, Walcott's prodigious achievements – and the hero status they brought him in the West Indies – had the additional bonus of peeling away any residual doubts there may have been in British Guiana about the value of having him as the country's cricket organiser. After all, if the young players on the sugar estates were unable to take anything from the best player in the world, then who could they learn from? By contrast to the fractious England series of the previous year, Australia's visit to the West Indies was mainly sweetness and light, and although the home side lost, Walcott enjoyed the ambience of the matches, as well as the off-field camaraderie with a set of hard-nosed but companionable opposition players.

If there was any discord this time, it was to be found inside the West Indies dressing room, where the captaincy issue was continuing to gnaw away at its insides. With captain John Goddard unavailable, the West Indies Cricket Board of Control had again sidestepped the competing claims of Walcott, Weekes and Worrell by appointing two light-skinned players as captain and vice-captain, the Trinidadian Jeff Stollmeyer and the Barbadian Denis Atkinson.

Stollmeyer was by now a seasoned campaigner with 30 Tests under his belt, but Atkinson was much more undercooked, with just 11 Tests to his name – and with not much of a record of achievement either. And yet Atkinson, the same age as Walcott, had also already been named as captain for the upcoming tour to New Zealand in early 1956, with another white man, Bruce Pairaudeau (seven Tests), chosen as his deputy for that trip. 'The public were not slow to ask why the three Ws had been left out of the reckoning', Walcott recalled,[2] the popular perception being that the board 'did not relish the prospect of having a coloured captain'.[3]

In public, Walcott, diplomatic as ever, preferred to put the situation down to class, rather than race. Pointing out that Goddard, Stollmeyer, Atkinson and Pairaudeau were all amateurs, he argued that the board was 'following the old-fashioned precedent of standing out against the professional captain',[4] a position the English authorities had clung on to until only just recently. Although there was something in that argument, it conveniently overlooked the fact that it was the white players' privileged racial positions that had allowed them to maintain their amateur status in the first place. And regardless of amateur or professional standing, it would have been inconceivable for a white player of Walcott's stature to have been overlooked for the captaincy of the West Indies. 'It was ridiculous that Denis Atkinson, fine character that he was, was appointed before the three Ws during that 1955 tour', concluded Benaud.[5]

Whatever the reasons behind the board's decisions, the festering issue of the captaincy hardly helped to promote cohesion in the West Indies side, even if most of the individuals within it – Walcott included – tried to put it to the back of their minds. To make things worse, Stollmeyer picked up injuries during the series, leaving the inexperienced Atkinson to skipper the team in the first, fourth and fifth Tests, while the captain himself could only take charge in the second and third matches. Leadership was not the main reason for the West Indies' 3–0 defeat – essentially that was down to a weak bowling attack, with Worrell forced to take the new ball in three of the Tests – but Atkinson's presence at the helm in the majority of the matches prompted sections of the Caribbean press to renew their call for a deserving black captain to take on the role.

In most instances the newspapers' choice was Worrell, not Walcott – for Worrell had actually been vice-captain for the 1953–54 series against England. But there is little doubt that if Walcott had been chosen in his stead, then there would have been few dissenters – and that Worrell himself would have backed him to the hilt. Despite some suggestions that the competing captaincy ambitions of Worrell and Walcott interfered with the smooth-running of their relationship, Walcott always maintained that this was not so, pointing out that during the 1955 series against Australia, he roomed with Worrell or Weekes whenever possible. 'We were friends, not rivals', he said.[6] Worrell also insisted that 'we have always remained firm friends, there have been no petty jealousies, no cross words between us',[7] while close observers generally witnessed only good relations between the three. Brian Scovell maintained that 'they loved each other and were almost like brothers',[8] and while this may have been overstating the case, it certainly appears that although they were three ambitious men, they each buried their potential rivalries in the service of a higher cause.

Rather than look for any point of discord between Walcott and Worrell – or indeed Weekes – it would be more fruitful to emphasise that they each shared a legitimate recurring frustration over the captaincy, against a backdrop of widespread nationalist promptings. The three Ws, as David Woodhouse observes, 'supplied most of the batting power and a lot of the thinking power, but they were not in command of the side'.[9]

More specifically, Worrell had been overlooked for the captaincy for Australia's visit in 1955 despite his vice-captaincy during the previous home series against England, and even though the man who had captained him, Goddard, had momentarily stepped aside. While the board insisted that Worrell was not out of the running for the job at some point in the future, few could see how that was possible given the way things were going. The presence of Atkinson as captain against Australia was an 'insult' to Worrell, said Manley,[10] and as such was also a slight to his friends. 'Worrell could have been expected to understand being asked to serve under a Walcott or a Weekes', he said, 'but Atkinson had no such claim based on cricket'.[11]

The demoralising effect on Worrell naturally spread to Weekes and Walcott, and despite Walcott's Herculean efforts across the 1955 home series, he found it difficult to swim away from the underlying current of disaffection that had become increasingly strong since the 1951–52 tour to Australia. Both he and Worrell, though they were loath to reveal as much in public, now had a simmering anger at having been obliged to play under a series of white captains whom they felt were inferior candidates for the job.

This demotivation fed into a prevailing mood of passive resistance towards the captain, as had happened with Goddard against Australia in 1951–52 – nothing personal, but certainly political, with a small p. For Walcott and Worrell it also helped to bring about a change in priorities, as evidenced by Walcott's decision to take up his work in British Guiana and Worrell's increasing focus on academic studies. While both courses of action reflected the fact that professional cricketers in those days were not served well by a game that offered little long-term security, the fact that they both began to think of other career paths at such an early point was also a reflection of their general state of disillusionment.

When asked if he would be available for the 1955–56 trip to New Zealand, Walcott, concerned about interference with his work in British Guiana and with reservations about the leadership of Atkinson, held off making a decision for so long that in the end the West Indies Board announced its squad without him, and so for the first time he missed an overseas tour with the team. Worrell was also unavailable, choosing instead to begin studies for a degree in administration at Manchester University in England. Having entered the most productive playing period of his career, Walcott therefore played no more Test cricket for almost two years, his next West Indies adventure arriving in the five-match series in England that began in May 1957.

Unusually, Muriel accompanied Walcott on that 1957 tour, although she did not join him immediately. Prior to Walcott's boat journey on the SS *Golfito* to England with the West Indies squad, they had taken their two children to stay with Walcott's parents in Barbados, and Muriel remained behind with them for a while before making her own separate way to England.

The opening few games of the tour were promising for Walcott, and he started off in the first Test at Edgbaston as if he had never been away, scoring an impressive 90 in the first innings. But in that innings he also tore a hamstring, scoring the last 40 runs with a runner. The injury would dog his performances for the rest of the campaign, and although across the trip he made some decent scores – finishing tenth in the first-class averages in England that summer (with 45.51) – over the remaining Tests he had a lean time of things, averaging just 27.44, with the 90 in Birmingham his sole Test half century. Out of action for two weeks after the initial injury, he had to receive injections just to be able to play in the second Test, and was under the attention of the physio for much of the rest of the trip.

He also had concerns about his back, which although much better since he had given up wicketkeeping, was always a potential threat to his wellbeing. In an effort to take the pressure off his spine, Walcott's batting stance had been much adjusted from his early days, when he stood up to his full height with straight legs. Now he adopted a more crouched position, allowing his bent legs to take some of the strain off his back. Conscious of the vulnerability of his leg and his back during the England tour, it is little wonder that his form failed to return after the first Test.

Walcott was not alone in his batting troubles, however: Weekes, who had serious sinus problems that made breathing difficult, finished with an even worse Test average of 19.50 over the tour, and in general the West Indies, with a number of new players in the team, struggled to assert themselves against a strong England outfit that featured Fred Trueman, Brian Statham, Jim Laker and Tom Graveney. Crucially, England's middle-order pairing of Peter May and Colin

Cowdrey also put an end to Sonny Ramadhin's effect-iveness with a turnaround stand of 411 in the second innings of the first Test in which Ramadhin was forced to bowl a shattering 98 overs as the home side salvaged an unlikely draw. Walcott felt that May and Cowdrey's use of the pads to kick away many of Ramadhin's deliv-eries was a dubious, if legal, tactic, but acknowledged that it was an effective one and felt that the West Indies never recovered from the dramatic reverse of fortune it brought about. Thereafter England were the better side throughout the series, and the West Indies punched well below their weight, losing 3–0.

Beyond that, however, once again the captaincy issue had dogged the series for the visitors, affecting morale and performance. Goddard, who had played little Test cricket since 1952, had regained his leader-ship position for the tour and this time Walcott, who had recently captained British Guiana to victory in the domestic quadrangular tournament, was handed the vice-captaincy.

Although that move might have been interpreted as some kind of progress for advocates of black leader-ship, there is little doubt that Walcott would have felt conflicted about his vice-captaincy. On the passage to England, he and the other black professionals had been accommodated in steerage class, while Goddard and the white amateurs (Goddard, Atkinson, Bruce Pairaudeau and Gerry Alexander) travelled in luxury cabins.[12] Having long since decided that he would provide only limited support to the leaders who had been foisted upon him, now Walcott was in the invidious position of having to provide close back-up to Goddard as his deputy.

While there is little evidence of personal animosity between Walcott and Goddard, there was almost inevitably an underlying tension based on their unequal status. How much of this was down to race and how much to class is a moot point. Ivo Tennant has suggested that while Goddard was happy in Walcott's company, in the general run of things he would not normally associate with cricketers of a lower social status, of whatever race.

The consequences of the disconnect between Goddard and Walcott were serious. 'It turned out to be a disastrous tour, one of the most miserable ever undertaken by a West Indies side', said Walcott later.[13] 'Goddard was not worth his place and it soon became obvious that the balance of the side was affected by having to play him.'[14] More than that, the skipper's tactical limitations were regularly exposed: he had virtually no rapport with the younger members of the squad, discipline declined – especially in the area of fielding – and he was unable to keep the team together in any meaningful way. On the 1950 tour of England Walcott had been young and relatively inexperienced, and was happy to be of help to Goddard; this time he was not going to give him the same kind of assistance.

As early as June, Alf Gover in the *Sunday Pictorial* was suggesting that Goddard, struggling for batting form, was thinking about stepping aside to let Walcott captain the side in the second Test at Lord's. But in the end he decided to soldier on. In short order a number of papers were reporting rumours that Walcott and Goddard were not seeing eye to eye, and that as vice-captain Walcott was not giving his skipper the support he needed. Later, Stratton Smith of the *Daily Sketch* even went so far as to say that the touring party had become 'entrenched in gloom' because of 'an absolute lack of confidence in the leadership'.[15]

With the team visibly split into groups, at least to the media, there were rumours that Atkinson had briefed against the three Ws for their unseemly interest in earning money, and there was further upset when the (white Guyanese) joint tour manager, Cecil de Caires, suggested to the press that Walcott was not making enough effort to get back to full fitness from his injury.

While Walcott denied any suggestions that he was undermining his skipper, it appears that his relationship with Goddard was certainly strained. Furthermore, even the impression that this was the case was bound to be harmful to Walcott in terms of how he was regarded by the powers that be.

Walcott himself later said that de Caires seemed to be suspicious that he was angling to undermine Goddard for his own ends, and the rumours swirling around about internal discontent were hardly useful in enhancing his credentials as a potential leader. As an added complication, Walcott's acceptance of the vice-captaincy may also have interfered temporarily with his relationship with Worrell, who had not so long ago been vice-captain himself, and who now appeared to be behind his friend in the pecking order to become the first permanent black captain of the West Indies. 'I thought Frank Worrell was the obvious choice, and so did the rest of the players', said Walcott.[16] But having been handed the job he had to get on with it.

Despite the strained relationship with Goddard, as well as suggestions in some quarters (including by Tennant) that he 'did not pull his weight',[17] there is no tangible evidence that Walcott failed to carry out his new responsibilities anything but seriously, or to the best of his ability. During the tour he took on full captaincy duties in nine first-class matches, winning five of them (including against Derbyshire, Surrey and Kent) and drawing the other four. He was also unbeaten as the stand-in captain in three other non-first-class matches on tour. Despite that good record, however, his vice-captaincy was not generally seen as a success.

One reason for this may have been his misfortune in being handed the reins during the final Test at the Oval, where Goddard came down with influenza at the end of the first day. With the series already comfortably lost and the pattern of defeat set, morale was at rock-bottom, and there was nothing much Walcott could do to stem the tide.

Bowled out for 89 and 86, the West Indies' tired players were defeated by an innings and 237 runs, with 16 wickets taken by Tony Lock and Laker on a powdery, turning pitch. It was the first time Walcott had captained the West Indies, and he had presided over a capitulation.

By contrast, just before the Oval Test, with both Goddard and Walcott indisposed, Worrell had taken on the captaincy for a match against Leicestershire, which the West Indies had won by an innings. After the final Test Worrell also took on two end-of-season games, winning against an L. E. G. Ames' XI and drawing with Lancashire. John Arlott, among a number of English commentators, saw a marked difference between Worrell and Walcott in charge, noting that while Worrell 'made an impressive mark'[18] with his 'manner and performance',[19] Walcott had generally failed to do so. Manley also concluded that 'Walcott had been less than a success as vice-captain but Worrell had proven himself in a leadership capacity'.[20]

In a sense, then, Worrell had been able to stay usefully above the fray on the England tour, while Walcott, in his official capacity as vice-captain, had been handed a poisoned chalice – working with, but unable to fully support, a leader he did not approve of. Inevitably, some of the blame for a poor series was laid at Walcott's door, and the situation was made worse because injury problems and poor form had prevented him from making much of an ameliorating contribution with the bat. By contrast, Worrell was the only one of the three Ws to have a relatively good time out in the middle. Though he hardly hit the heights, he at least averaged 38.88 in the Tests, scored a majestic unbeaten 191 at Nottingham in the third Test to salvage a draw, and in all matches averaged 58.80, putting him into fifth spot in the 1957 English first-class averages. By the end of the tour, if anyone was going to be a future black captain, then it was going to be Worrell and not Walcott.

On his return to British Guiana via Barbados, after staying on for a period of study at the Industrial Welfare Society during the latter part of 1957, Walcott was a chastened and rather disappointed man. It was all rather different from the triumphs of England in 1950. 'This time there was no grand welcome', he reflected.[21] 'I was elected one of Wisden's five Cricketers of the Year for 1957 and I can only imagine it was for past achievements prior to the first Test in England.'[22] Goddard had played his last Test, and for Walcott it was the beginning of the end, too.

When the home series against Pakistan came up the following year (1958), it was Worrell and not Walcott who was offered the captaincy. Worrell, however, was in the middle of his degree studies and was compelled to turn the offer down – an outcome the selectors must surely have expected. Rather than then turning to Walcott, the selectors ignored him completely, instead handing the leadership to the light-skinned Jamaican wicketkeeper Gerry Alexander, who had played just two Test matches up to that point and had never captained any first-class side.

Walcott, therefore, had now fallen not only beneath Worrell in the pecking order, but below a two-cap ingenu with a Test batting average of 3.7, whose only first-class matches prior to the England tour of 1957 had been with Cambridge University in 1952 and 1953. To make matters worse, he was not even appointed vice-captain, losing his say in selection as a result.

'Following Goddard's ... catastrophic leadership of England in 1957, the popular perception was that it was opportune for one of the three Ws to captain the West Indies – that in keeping with the political advance towards Federation [of the West Indies] and the likelihood of independence, the time had come for a black captain to lead the regional team', says Seecharan.[23] The selectors, notwithstanding their initial offer to Worrell, seemed to have other ideas. Somehow, neither Walcott nor Weekes were considered suitable.

Ironically, Walcott's professional status could no longer be used as an excuse to sidestep him, as he had recently been told by the West Indies Board that they now regarded him as an amateur, due to his work on the sugar estates in British Guiana. Notwithstanding the fact that his vice-captaincy on the 1957 England tour had been tainted by association with failure, the only possible reason for ignoring Walcott this time was his skin colour.

'Clyde could no longer be deemed a professional ... so he could not conceivably have been overlooked on that premise', says Seecharan.[24] 'Therefore it was widely assumed that the inexperienced Alexander was awarded the captaincy because of his Cambridge education, coupled with the fact that he was perceived as white or near white.'[25]

Whatever the internal reasons for choosing Alexander, the West Indies public certainly thought it was due to the colour of his skin. 'It was not a fair decision because either Weekes or Walcott, magnificent players for the West Indies over a decade, merited the post before Alexander', says Seecharan.[26] 'But the board was still primarily an institution in which white or very light men ruled the roost. They were probably unconsciously still swayed by narrow ethnic proclivities.'[27]

Even Alexander could not understand the decision, though he was in no real position to turn down the job. 'I thought the great injustice of my appointment against Pakistan was not primarily to Frank Worrell but to Clyde Walcott and Everton Weekes', he told the Australian cricket writer Mike Coward in 2000.[28] The Guyanese cricketer Ivan Madray, who played two Tests in the series against Pakistan, put it more starkly: 'Imagine a team being captained by this incompetent novice, Alexander, while this great man, Walcott, looked on', he said.[29]

In pure cricketing terms, the high-scoring five-Test home series against Pakistan was an immeasurably better one for Walcott. Although he missed the second Test when his back problems flared up again, he managed to amass 385 runs from the five innings he played, scoring 43, 88, 145, 47 and 62 as the West Indies won 3–1. His century – the fifteenth and last of his career – came during the West Indies' eight-wicket victory in the fourth Test in Georgetown, and his average across the series was 96.25. Wisden reported that he and Weekes played with all their old mastery.

However, at the end of the series Walcott announced that he had decided to retire from Test cricket – at the age of 32. Weekes, a year older, made a similar declaration. Both appeared to have taken as much as they could handle of the serial disappointments and machinations within the West Indies set-up – Walcott, in particular, was 'tired of intrigues and manoeuvres which were not based on cricket ability', according to C. L. R. James.[30]

Clearly Walcott had much more to give to the West Indies. Although Pakistan were a middling side, he had demonstrated great consistency against their bowling attack, and after the injury-hit aberration of the 1957 England tour was back to something near his best – in fact James felt he was 'batting at the peak',[31] with a 'physique [that] is still one of the most powerful in cricket'.[32] Yet at the end of the final Test at Port of Spain, in March 1958, he returned to the sugar estates of British Guiana with no thoughts of playing international cricket again.

Back in Georgetown there were no first-class matches for Walcott until January 1959, when he played the first of three inter-colonial games for British Guiana. England toured the West Indies in 1960, but his only scheduled involvement was to be captain of British Guiana against the touring side in Georgetown, a drawn four-day match in which he made a rapid 83 in his only innings.

By then, three Tests of the tour had already taken place in Barbados, Trinidad and Jamaica, and the West Indies, missing Walcott's quick scoring in the middle order, were 1–0 down. Various parties – including James, who had 'begged him to come back, in person, through friends, [and] by overseas telephone'[33] – attempted to persuade him to rethink his retirement. Then, with the next Test to be played on his 'home' territory in British Guiana, the board invited Walcott to come back on professional terms for the final two Tests, and he agreed to the deal. Much to the disappointment of the locals in British Guiana, in his only innings in Georgetown Walcott scored 9, and although in the final Test at Port of Spain he posted more respectable scores of 53 and 22, he was unable to help the West Indies level the series, which remained at 1–0 to England.

Walcott's return to international cricket for the back end of that series did not, however, presage a change of heart. He had happened to be around in a moment of need, was paid for his trouble, and had no intention of making a comeback of greater duration. Having scored 3,798 runs in 44 Tests at an average of 56.68, he had played his final Test match.

As it happened, the 1960–61 tour to Australia might have been an ideal opportunity for Walcott to make a return. During the England tour of the West Indies in 1960, as independence for Trinidad, Barbados, Jamaica and British Guiana was edging ever closer, the failure to appoint a black captain had become increasingly untenable. Although Alexander had developed into a decent leader over three series (at home to Pakistan in 1958, away in India and Pakistan in 1958–59 and at home to England in 1960), by the end of 1959 Worrell had finished his degree studies and was finally in a position to take on the job. Alexander, suffering from what he called 'Worrelitis' – the public hostility directed his way because he was 'blocking' the great man – was only too happy to stand aside in Worrell's favour and to be his deputy in Australia.

Worrell asked Walcott to play on the 1960–61 tour to Australia, but he declined. Although his reasons for standing down in 1958 had probably been more to do with the politics of West Indies cricket – especially in relation to the captaincy – he had continued to have difficulties with his back, and the brief return against England had shown that success with the bat was far from guaranteed. Besides, he was also now more heavily involved in his duties as social welfare organiser in British Guiana, with wider responsibilities than before. 'I had no regrets about retiring', he said later[34]. 'I felt it was the right time.'[35]

Nonetheless he was still only 34, and it was a terrible waste for the West Indies to lose his talents at that age. It was also a great personal shame for Walcott, who, as C. L. R. James said, 'put big cricket behind him'[36] at 'the height of his powers'.[37] There was little evidence that Walcott's proficiency was waning significantly, and it would surely have been liberating for him to have played a final series or two under Worrell. At last he would have been able to play with complete commitment to the cause and in a side that was free of simmering internal dissatisfaction.

Worrell's drawn series in Australia was happy and highly successful – one of the most celebrated tours of all time and, with hindsight, Walcott must surely

**Figure 5.1** 1994 card in the Cricketing Knights series (No. 5), printed in England.

have regretted that he did not take part. A new-look West Indies side had emerged under Alexander in the previous three years, featuring the burgeoning young talents of Garfield Sobers, Wes Hall, Conrad Hunte and Collie Smith, along with Walcott's four Guyanese 'finds', Basil Butcher, Rohan Kanhai, Lance Gibbs and Joe Solomon, all of whom he would have been able to help flower still further if he had been in the side.

Once Worrell finally became the first regular black captain of the West Indies, the transformation in the outlook of the team was immediate and dramatic. Released from decades of uptight introspection about the captaincy issue, West Indies players could at last begin to pull in the same direction. With Alexander at his side as loyal lieutenant, Worrell's inclusive, relaxed style of leadership – in stark contrast to the rather aloof colonial-era captaincy of some of those who had preceded him – created the happy, sporting atmosphere that Walcott had so often craved. Worrell pursued adventurous, attacking cricket while playing the game in the 'true spirit' that both he and Walcott had learned about at Combermere.

Might that have been Walcott's style, too, had he become the first permanent black captain of the West Indies – as he should have done in 1958? Worrell and Walcott differed in personality, but they shared many values, and it would be safe to assume that their approach might have been similar. There would certainly have been the same inclusiveness: 'Clyde

Walcott and Frank Worrell were two of the biggest men I ever knew: they had no time for race, pettiness or spite', said Madray.[38] 'They were highly cultured men, who took a man for what he was worth.'[39] Walcott proved in his work on the sugar plantations – and as captain of British Guiana – that he had no time for insularity or restricted thinking.

Their relaxed attitude to leadership was also a shared characteristic: at one of his seminars for aspiring cricketers in British Guiana in 1963, Walcott had told his audience that a captain 'must try to cultivate and show an evenness of temper: he must be composed and, however desperate the situation, his team must never be allowed to sense that their captain is rattled'.[40] Walcott would also have offered the same supportive, nurturing approach that Worrell adopted; he had shown that quality in spades in British Guiana, including in the way he had brought along the likes of Kanhai, Butcher and Solomon.

There would, though, have been differences. While they were two men of easy charm, Worrell was the more flamboyant and charismatic of the pair, and it is questionable whether under Walcott's leadership things would have been quite so relaxed. Worrell had a greater lightness of touch, could socialise more easily with his players (often through the medium of drink), and would speak to them individually on matters beyond cricket, while still maintaining a high level of respect. By contrast, Walcott was an altogether more staid character who, being essentially a non-drinker, was hampered in his ability to interact with colleagues on a more informal level. Even though Walcott had looked a more likely captaincy candidate for much of the earlier parts of their careers, Worrell was emphatically the right man for the job at the right time and, as a more visibly political figure, it was beneficial that he took on the captaincy just as the West Indies territories began to emerge from colonial rule.

Whatever the merits and demerits of both men, however, Walcott should certainly have been provided with a shot at the captaincy. Given what he went on to achieve in other aspects of the game, it is barely conceivable that he would have failed to be an effective leader of the West Indies. Had Walcott been appointed in 1958, he may well have voluntarily stepped aside for Worrell when the time came, and the West Indies would have had profitable years' service from both of them.

That there was such concerted manipulation to exclude all three Ws from leadership, for so long, was a severe indictment of the way cricket was run in the West Indies, and a sore waste of talent. Having been frustrated in his leadership ambitions on the field, Walcott would have to seek opportunities in other directions.

# 6

# Steering the West Indies
# to greatness

Although Walcott retired from Test matches in 1960, he continued to play first-class cricket for British Guiana until 1964. In October 1961 he had captained the side to victory against Barbados in the final of a reconfigured regional pentangular tournament, which for the first time included the combined Leeward and Windward Islands. His next match was not until February 1963, against Barbados, when he led the team to another victory, also appearing in two first-class games later in the year at the Machado cricket festival in Jamaica, where he played first for The Rest (captained by Everton Weekes) against a West Indies XI, scoring 82 in the first innings, and then for a Frank Worrell XI against C. C. Hunte's XI, for whom he compiled 105 in the second innings.

In the regional tournament of 1964 – which was back after a period in abeyance, and reduced again to just four teams – Walcott missed British Guiana's first, drawn match against Barbados in February, then captained the side to an innings victory against Jamaica at Georgetown and a draw at the same venue against Trinidad, results that were enough to give British Guiana the title again. That match, which ended on 14 March 1964, proved to be his final first-class encounter at the age of 38.

Between 1955 and 1964 Walcott had played 16 matches for British Guiana, scoring 911 runs at an average of 43.48. From 1956 onwards he was captain in 12 matches, delivering eight wins, four draws and just two defeats as he transformed the team into the best side in the Caribbean. British Guiana won all three of the regional tournaments available to him when he was captain.

Walcott's first-class career outside Test cricket was truncated by modern standards, and he certainly appeared in many fewer games than any English or Australian player of his era would have expected during a career of the same length. For logistical and organisational reasons, the number of first-class games available to West Indian players from the late 1940s to the early 1960s was very limited, and in fact Walcott played fewer matches for Barbados and British Guiana (41) than he did Tests for the West Indies (55). Before becoming a British Guiana player, he had appeared just 25 times for Barbados over the 12-year period from 1942 to 1954, with a batting average of 58.20 and 16 wickets at 25.56 apiece.

# Clyde Walcott

The most significant number of Walcott's 102 first-class matches (excluding Tests) came in 44 games for the West Indies during tour encounters against English counties, Australian state, and Indian and Pakistani representative sides, while there were a handful of other matches for ad hoc representative teams, including two for a Commonwealth XI in England in 1953 at the back end of his penultimate Enfield season. In all first-class matches outside of Test cricket, Walcott scored 8,022 runs at an average of 56.49 from 142 completed innings.

Even when Test cricket is added into the equation, Walcott's batting average was remarkably similar: his 11,820 runs in all 146 games of his 22-year career came at an average of 56.55, with 40 centuries. In Test cricket on its own, the figure was virtually the same: 56.68, with 3,798 runs and 15 hundreds. Those figures speak of an incredibly consistent talent – and an outstanding one too, given that a career average of more than 50 is generally considered a mark of greatness.

Although Walcott's top-line cricket came to an end in early 1964, he did not turn his back on the game altogether. He continued to play local inter-county and club matches into the late 1960s (including for the Georgetown Cricket Club in the Case Cup), and from 1968 to 1970 was president of the Cricket Board of Control in Guyana, effectively in charge of all cricket in the country – a post that gave him a position as one of the West Indies Test selectors. Although he was by then a social welfare organiser for the SPA, he maintained a keen interest in sugar plantation cricket, and was a useful mentor to Joe Solomon, who was by now serving in Walcott's previous role as SPA cricket organiser.

By 1970, however, the attraction of Guyana had begun to wane. Severe economic hardship had hit the country as Forbes Burnham's increasingly dictatorial and violent regime began to align itself with the Soviet Union, Cuba and North Korea, banning imports, nationalising industries and starting to clamp down on press freedom. It is unclear what sympathy, if any, Walcott had nurtured for Burnham's Afro-Guyanese PNC government when it first emerged, but if he did have any, then it was certainly not enough to keep him in the country as events took a turn for the worse in the final years of the 1960s. By 1969 he was, in his own words 'hankering to return to Barbados',[1] and as a consequence began to put out feelers about work openings in his homeland.

One of those feelers went in the direction of Anthony Murray, a well-connected English owner of the island's Kendal sugar plantation, who was able to persuade the chief personnel officer of the Barbados Shipping and Trading Company to interview Walcott for the post of personnel officer. The interview went well, Walcott accepted the position, and after 16 years in Guyana he moved back to Barbados with Muriel, Michael and Ian, settling in the Wildey area of Bridgetown on its eastern edge.

Walcott's new employer was one of the largest companies on the island, with 3,000 staff members and,
aside from its main activity of shipping and trading,
fingers in a number of pies, including manufacturing,
insurance and property management. The move suited
Walcott, involving him in negotiations on behalf of
the company with trade union representatives, something that chimed naturally with his previous work in
Guyana, where personnel work had been important.
Undoubtedly his cricketing fame would have oiled
the wheels of the negotiations he took part in, providing him with a degree of familiarity and respect –
not to say a wealth of ice-breaking informal talking
points about cricket – with union leaders. The work
also prepared him for later managerial work in cricket,
notably with the sport's global governing body, the
International Cricket Council (ICC).

After eight years as a personnel officer Walcott
was elected president of the Barbados Employers'
Confederation, a voluntary position he held alongside his company job until relinquishing it in 1981,
by which time he had risen to become chief personnel
officer at Barbados Shipping and Trading, as well as an
executive director – the first black man to be appointed
to such a position. He remained in post until 1991, and
from 1982 to 1987 was also a member of the Barbados
Public Service Commission, a small committee of
appointees tasked with advising the government on
personnel issues.

Aside from the career possibilities that Walcott's new employment offered, his post with Barbados Shipping and Trading also allowed him time off for cricketing duties if and when the need arose, for his new employers were sympathetic to any voluntary work in that direction. Thus began a number of years in which Walcott became the manager of various West Indies tours, accepting the role on an expenses-only basis and usually having to forfeit his four weeks' annual company leave in the process.

The year before his arrival back in Barbados, Walcott had set this trend in motion by accepting a first offer to manage the West Indies on their brief, three-Test 1969 series in England, with the Barbadian Peter Short as his assistant manager and treasurer. Walcott had been given time off from his SPA work to do so, and arrived in England with the side in late April. The West Indies team he managed, now under the captaincy of Garfield Sobers, was a relatively weak one, and the tour, played in wet and cold weather, ended in a 2–0 series defeat. Seymour Nurse, Rohan Kanhai, Conrad Hunte, Wes Hall and Charlie Griffith were all absent, while many of the squad were relative newcomers, putting a huge burden on the shoulders of Lance Gibbs and Basil Butcher, big beasts from a more successful era who were coming to the end of their careers. A great deal of responsibility also fell on Sobers, who was exhausted and injury-prone after a long period of more or less continuous cricket. England, by contrast, were a strong outfit under the captaincy of Ray Illingworth, featuring the likes of John Snow, Derek Underwood, Alan Knott, Basil D'Oliveira, John Edrich and Geoffrey Boycott.

Although his admiration for Sobers knew no bounds, Walcott realised during the trip that his captain had too much on his plate, and that the side were overly dependent on him. 'He was too great a cricketer to be a captain because he always expected everyone to perform as he did, and that was not possible', he said.[2] 'One problem with Gary's captaincy was that, when things were going badly, he would come on to bowl himself. He expected things to happen every time he was involved in the action.'[3]

There were only three victories across the 22 first-class matches on the three-month trip, which also included a humiliating defeat on a horribly wet wicket in a non-first-class fixture against Ireland at Sion Mills in which Walcott, stepping in at the age of 43 to give Sobers a rest, was second highest scorer in a total of 25 all out.

Walcott deemed the tour results 'acutely disappointing',[4] but was sanguine about the general outcome, acknowledging that team spirit was good, that a rebuilding process was under way and that 'it was a useful learning exercise for the younger players'.[5] There were bright spots, with three Guyanese – Butcher, Clive Lloyd and Roy Fredericks – all performing well, and Walcott was at least able to work on his management skills with the youngsters.

One notable success, he believed, was with Fredericks, who was known at that point for producing stylish 30s and 40s before getting out prematurely. As a man who had been a committed smoker for many years, Walcott identified that Fredericks's heavy intake of cigarettes was a possible cause of his lack of stamina, and the younger man took his manager's advice to cut back dramatically, improving his fitness and prolonging his stints at the crease as a result. Even at that early stage, Walcott's philosophy as a manager – built up, he said, through his earlier training in England at the Industrial Welfare Society – was 'to chastise in private and praise in public',[6] always making sure he never criticised a player while anyone else was in earshot.

As well as being manager, Walcott was one of five selectors on the 1969 England tour, each representing a different West Indies territory. Always an opponent of parochialism, soon afterwards he managed to persuade Jeff Stollmeyer, president of the West Indies Board, to reduce the size of the selection committee to three members on future tours, arguing that not only would this be a more manageable size, but that without members representing specific territories there would be less likelihood of them each pressing for the inclusion of players from their own domain. The change proved to be one of the foundations for future West Indies success, and Walcott felt that it encouraged players to regard themselves as playing for their 'nation' of Caribbean states rather than just trying to please their compatriots back home with a good performance.

With three consecutive home series to follow, Walcott's main cricketing focus over the next three years was on his selectorial duties. The chief difficulty during that period was the fitness and availability of Sobers, most notably during the 1973 home series against the Australians, during which Walcott also took on management duties for the West Indies team. By that time Sobers, who was trying to manage his body over a punishing year-round schedule that included county cricket for Nottinghamshire, had undergone a second operation on his knee.

Walcott was deputed to talk to the captain about his fitness ahead of the series, and Sobers told him that he thought he might be ready for the second Test. Walcott, it appears, was happy to take Sobers' experienced word on the matter, but Stollmeyer, as chairman of selectors and board president, insisted that he should undergo a formal fitness test and practice match before any recall, and asked Walcott to relay the message. When Walcott did so, Sobers, feeling the idea betrayed a lack of trust of his integrity and judgement, lost his temper and decided that it was better to withdraw from the series altogether.

The public and political fallout from the spat was considerable in the West Indies, for Sobers was the best player in the world and the series was subsequently lost 2–0. His non-appearance was even raised at the heads of government conference in Guyana, where Eric Williams, prime minister of Trinidad, criticised the manner in which the selectors had handled the issue, accusing them of discarding Sobers like 'an old car that has been smashed up in a road accident'.[7] Walcott admitted later that the series had consequently been a 'fraught' one for him, and while he never said so specifically, some of his later comments suggested he did not wholly agree with Stollmeyer's hard-line stance. If Walcott's inclination to go with Sobers' gut feeling had prevailed, then the captain would probably have played two or three matches. Instead he finished up playing none.

During that series Walcott also had a taste of attempted political interference in selection policy when the Guyanese prime minister, Forbes Burnham, successfully intervened to get Clive Lloyd released from his contract with South Melbourne cricket club in Australia, and then paid for him to be flown home to the West Indies in the hope that he would not only be selected for the side but might become the West Indies captain in Sobers' absence. However, Kanhai was chosen as skipper and Lloyd, who was going through a short period of indifferent form, did not even make the team for the first Test in Jamaica. When he was left out for the second Test in Barbados as well, he reacted in uncharacteristically peevish fashion, smashing a ball through a dressing-room window and refusing to be twelfth man in the match.

'He felt he had been victimised because he was sponsored by his government [but] I sat him down and told him he had a great future, possibly as West Indies captain, and urged him not to throw everything away on a false belief', said Walcott.[8] 'We were not concerned that his prime minister was pushing him.'[9] The chat pulled Lloyd back into the fold, and in the event he was selected for the last three Tests of the series, during which he not only made 178 in Georgetown but also opened the bowling in two matches.

Although Walcott was an enthusiastic supporter of Kanhai as captain, his timely intervention to reassure Lloyd about his future leadership credentials proved to be a key moment in a particularly close and pro-ductive relationship with the man who later led the West Indies to world dominance. 'He comforted me, he knew me from home, he'd been my first captain and he said "You have a great part to play in West Indies cricket"', said Lloyd later.[10] 'I can't really describe how important his words were. What he said really made me change my whole way of thinking. Before then I just wanted to finish with cricket; I didn't want to play for the West Indies again. And his words proved to be prophetic.'[11]

Kanhai took over permanently from Sobers on the three-Test tour of England during the summer of 1973, which was Walcott's second stint as manager of a West Indies side abroad. Sobers made the best of his new-found freedom, averaging 76.50 with the bat as the

West Indies won the series 2–0, and this time there was little discord between player and selectors, perhaps because Walcott had by then taken on the role of chairman of selectors from Stollmeyer – a post he would hold, on and off, for the next 15 years. Walcott and his committee stuck with Kanhai as leader for the drawn home series against England in 1974, and were ready to go with him again for the 1974–75 tour to India and Pakistan, despite his relatively advanced age of 40. However, the West Indies Board made an unusual decision to overrule the selectors, going instead for 30-year-old Lloyd as captain and putting an end to Kanhai's Test career.

Walcott was unconvinced about the move initially, but observed that while Lloyd's captaincy 'was lacking in several departments'[12] at first, with the help of the tour manager Gerry Alexander 'he matured very quickly'[13] and proved to be more popular with his players than his predecessor. Kanhai, Walcott felt, had been 'a sound captain, a good tactician and knowledgeable about the game',[14] but had been rather moody, and lacked a strong rapport with the rest of the team. In the end, he conceded, the board's decision to appoint Lloyd had been the correct one, and the reward was a 3–2 series win in India, plus two drawn Tests against Pakistan.

By that point a very promising West Indies side was beginning to emerge, with Fredericks and Gordon Greenidge opening the batting (the latter a controversial pick by Walcott, as he had largely been brought up in England), followed by Alvin Kallicharran, Viv Richards, Lloyd, Deryck Murray and the all-rounder Keith Boyce in the middle order. While the bowling was not as strong as it would later become, Vanburn Holder and Bernard Julien were effective seamers, and Andy Roberts had recently made his debut. Going into the inaugural World Cup in June 1975, things were definitely looking up – and Walcott was brought back to manage the side for the two-week tournament in England.

As with previous and subsequent tours, his approach as manager during that first World Cup was to keep a light hand on the tiller, trusting the players to regu-late themselves. He could put on a stern countenance very effectively, calling in any recalcitrant player for a private chat and a serious warning, after which the chances of a re-offence were slim. But in general he was relaxed about giving players a free rein off the pitch, as long as their performances were unaffected.

Indicative of this generally consensual, rather than disciplinarian, approach was his decision on the night before the World Cup final against Australia to ask the players, in a team meeting, for their views on what time they felt they should be going to bed. When one of the senior members of the squad, Lance Gibbs, blurted out that the tour committee had already decided that the curfew should be 11pm, a slightly embarrassed Walcott explained that he had been hoping to reach a consensus on the decision rather than just announce what had been agreed in private. Fortunately, in any case, the players accepted that 11pm was a reasonable deadline and everyone was on time in the morning, which turned into a beautiful summer's day.

The West Indies' thrilling victory in that tense Lord's final, thanks to a lightning Lloyd century, four wickets from Boyce and three run-outs engineered by Richards, was a landmark moment in world cricket – a heady day for Walcott, Lloyd and their men but also for the cricketing authorities, who had hit upon a novel tournament idea that had become an immediate success. 'It might not be termed first-class cricket, but the game has never produced better entertainment in one day', said Wisden.[15] In the final moments there was a jubilant pitch invasion from the strong Caribbean contingent in the crowd, wonderfully reminiscent of the scenes after the great Victory Test at Lord's in which Walcott had played such a big part 25 years previously. Here he was again at the heart of the action, helping to guide the West Indies to one of their greatest moments.

As chairman of selectors Walcott had also championed the idea of picking the West Indies' best players for the tournament, rather than those who might be considered better one-day specialists. In those early beginnings of one-day international cricket this went against the grain of general thinking, for England and Australia in particular had favoured the selection of supposed one-day experts. 'There might be the odd cricketer who excels in the short form of cricket and is not so successful in Test matches, but in the main I believe you have to stick with your best players, and I think we were proved right to do so', Walcott said.[16] He was also proud of his decision to bring back Kanhai, who showed how good he was in the one-day game format with a crucial 55 in the final.

Walcott's personnel work in Barbados precluded him from making any commitment to manage the long 1975–76 tour to Australia, which turned out to be a chastening experience for Lloyd and his World Cup champions as they succumbed 5–1 to a strong Aussie side. But after a home series win against India in the spring of 1976, he was back in the management seat for the West Indies' trip to England in the summer of 1976, which proved to be the beginning of a golden period of dominance for the team.

With Andy Roberts, Wayne Daniel and Michael Holding now in the bowling line-up, the West Indies finally had a fine pace attack to complement their batting riches. They were also given a psychological gee-up on the eve of the first Test with a spectacularly misjudged BBC interview in which the home team's captain, Tony Greig, suggested that England would be aiming to make the visitors 'grovel'. In public, on the day after Grieg's interview, Walcott tried diplomatically to play down the remark, saying that it was 'just another of those psychological moves ... that are made before a big match'.[17] But in private he realised that it would have a significant galvanising effect on his men. 'To say that about West Indians, some of whose countries had only recently become independent from Britain, whose ancestors were slaves taken to the Caribbean from Africa, was an incredible gaffe', he said later.[18] 'What incensed [the players] even more was that Greig, although qualified to play for England through his parentage, was born in [apartheid] South Africa, brought up there and spoke with a South African accent. He was a straight-talking man but his choice of that word ... caused immense repercussions and had a telling effect on the outcome of the series.'[19]

The 'telling effect' was a crushing 3–0 victory for the visitors, with Richards scoring 829 runs at 118.42 and Holding and Roberts capturing 56 wickets between them at 12.71 and 19.17 apiece. There had been a changing of the guard within the West Indies ranks over the previous 12 months, with the likes of Sobers, Gibbs, Boyce and Kanhai now finally departed and a generation of younger players beginning to establish themselves. That managed transition had subjected Walcott to further public criticism as a selector, and he had privately told the players ahead of the England tour that he would be relinquishing his selectorial role. But they rallied round him and asked him to rethink. Boosted, and touched, by their vote of confidence, he decided to remain in position, launching himself into a new era characterised by a flowering of the relationship between himself, Lloyd and the players in general.

At that stage Lloyd still required a certain amount of practical and moral support from Walcott, although the skipper had learned valuable lessons in Australia in 1975–76 and was developing rapidly as a captain. During the course of a match, Walcott would be a regular presence in the dressing room but was careful not to overstep any boundaries. 'He would never be in there telling anyone what to do', says Michael Holding.[20] 'He left that to the captain, and I imagine that if he had any thoughts he relayed them privately to Clive, who would then decide whether to act on them or not. He had a very good relationship with Clive; there was clearly mutual respect, and while they worked together they also left each other to get on with their own jobs.'[21]

Known affectionately by the players as 'Manage', Walcott had a generally convivial relationship with his charges, although he made sure to hold them at the kind of distance needed to maintain discipline and control. 'Things were different in those days – you didn't go out with the manager socially or anything, which is often what happens these days', says Holding.

> It was a more hierarchical system, so that it was never a matter of him being pally-pally with any of the squad, although of course he had a bit of a closer relationship with some of the more seasoned players, people like Deryck Murray, Clive Lloyd and Roy Fredericks.
>
> Back then we had a manager, an assistant manager [Frank Thomas] and a baggage man. The assistant manager was the one organising what time the bus

left, dealing with meal allowances and so on – Clyde wouldn't get involved in any of that, it wasn't his job. And he wasn't a track suit manager either – it was the captain who led the practice sessions and the cricket side of things.

His main role was to be the official face of the West Indies team and Board. He was the one who made all the speeches and who spoke to the journalists, and he wouldn't allow the media to speak directly to any of the players, although the captain could do that. So he was our representative. During a game he would often be up in a box or a boardroom as an invited guest, and he was very good at that because he was an outgoing man. He seemed comfortable and relaxed in any environment.[22]

Despite his higher level of responsibilities as manager, Walcott would also voluntarily, and from time to time, take on a pastoral role with the players. Holding remembers being on the receiving end of his kind attention in England on that 1976 tour, when, as a 22-year-old novice, he found difficulty in keeping his footing on the unfamiliar green areas around the bowling crease during an early tour game at Southampton. 'I was slipping regularly and it felt very uncomfortable', he says.

It was the first time I was playing on an English surface like that, and I was just not accustomed to the soft ground. After the game, as we were on the way to the next venue, I was feeling a bit depressed about the situation and I put myself at the rear of the bus away from everybody.

Clyde was at the front with all the established players, but he noticed me at the back feeling sorry for myself and came to sit alongside me. I was shocked, and initially thought I'd done something wrong. But he just gently asked me what the problem was, and so I told him about my trouble with staying balanced at the crease, and that my boots didn't seem to be able to cope with the surface. He simply said: 'Speak to your friend Andy Roberts, I'm sure he can help you' and very soon afterwards Andy took me to a man in Northamptonshire who made me some fantastic boots with long studs, and I felt so much better.

He could sometimes be a little bit sarcastic and cutting, and that made some of the players a bit wary of him, but he was very well respected by everyone and he was a good, caring man. He would always be on the bus with us, he never travelled privately, and he was a real part of the squad.[23]

The 1976 England tour was the first in which the West Indies began to successfully experiment with a quartet of fast bowlers, and in his role as team spokesman Walcott bore the brunt of the criticism that accompanied that innovation, often having to be interrogated at length about its supposed unfairness. Some elements of the press corps were particularly relentless in their questioning of an accidental beamer bowled by Holding at Greig in the second Test at Lord's (for which Holding had apologised), and concerns were expressed in various quarters about the sustained hostility directed by Holding and Roberts towards two aged openers, John Edrich and Brian Close, in England's second innings of the third Test in Manchester. As Walcott did throughout the rest of his administrative career, he stoutly defended the use of what many regarded as intimidatory bowling, insisting that the short-pitched ball was a legitimate weapon in any cricketing arsenal. 'The journalists would not accept my contention that on a lively pitch the bowlers were entitled to bowl short occasionally, and that the use of the bouncer had not been overdone', he said.[24]

> Holding and Roberts were bowling a little short of a length [in Manchester] and, with their pace on that fast pitch the ball was rising more than is usually the case in a Test match in England. It was not a deliberate tactic to bully the English pair. Close was 45 and Edrich 37; their ages doubtless contributed to the criticism. But England's selectors had picked them because of their ability to play quick bowling. You cannot think of a batsman's age when you are playing against him in a Test match.[25]

Tellingly, while Walcott backed his bowlers to the hilt, he was privately rather annoyed that they had resorted to so much short stuff against Edrich and Close in that second innings – arguing that by pitching the ball further up they would probably have dismissed both of them much earlier. Under advice from Lloyd and Walcott, Holding, Roberts and Wayne Daniel bowled much more effectively in the later stages of that innings to deliver a thumping victory.

The second major innovation on the 1976 tour came off the field, with a new assertiveness among the West

Indies players in terms of their commercial worth. When the squad members announced that they were unwilling to attend any tour functions unless they were paid, Walcott, as an amateur administrator, was rather taken aback at the development, having previously regarded such events as 'a nice gesture' by the various companies involved. Nonetheless, he came to see the players' point of view, and supported them in their new stance.

Finances came to the fore more dramatically the following year (1977) with the launch of Kerry Packer's rebel World Series in Australia, which lured many of the world's best cricketers away from the official circuit. The West Indies Board took a more relaxed view of the World Series than some of cricket's other ruling bodies, but was under pressure from officials in England and Australia to hold the line against rebel players, who had taken large chunks of cash to play in unauthorised matches televised by Packer's Nine Network company.

Among the rebels were a sizeable number of West Indies players, including Lloyd, the vice-captain Murray, Richards, Holding and Roberts. Packer's negotiations to secure the West Indies players had gone ahead without Walcott's knowledge, and the announcement took him completely by surprise.

While the English and Australian rebels were banned from playing Tests by their own cricketing authorities, the West Indies selectors, with the support of their board, continued to pick Packer players for the home series against Australia in early 1978. However, when news arrived before the third Test that three more in the squad – Desmond Haynes, Colin Croft and Richard Austin – had signed up with Packer, the board began to worry about availability for the tour to India later that year. After it had unsuccessfully sought commitments on that front from various players, Walcott and his two fellow selectors, the chairman Joey Carew and John Holt, dropped Austin, Haynes and Deryck Murray for the third Test, prompting Lloyd, and all the other Packer players, to resign in solidarity.

Alvin Kallicharran was chosen as the new captain of a much-changed side, and the rest of the five Test rubber was played with a slew of unfamiliar figures, including Norbert Phillip, Sew Shivnarine and Derick Parry. The West Indies public generally sided with the rebels at this point, leading to small crowds for the final three games, which in any case were being played against a severely weakened Australia side. Although the West Indies won the series 3–1, the board lost money and was forced to send its new-look team under Kallicharran over to India for the 1978–79 series.

That depleted side did surprisingly well, losing the six-Test series only 1–0 against a strong Indian team. But shortly afterwards, in the spring of 1979, a world-wide truce with Packer was called, leading to the dis-bandment of World Series Cricket and the return of the West Indies defectors for the 1979–80 tour to Australia.

The Packer scenario had placed Walcott in an awkward position for the best part of two years, for while he sympathised with the rebel players – conceding that he would have taken the World Series money if he had been in the same situation – as an administrator and selector he was bound to do the board's bidding. He also felt that whatever the merits of the players' case, 'West Indies cricket had to look after itself'[26] or face extinction.

Although Walcott did not remotely buy into the idea that Packer's disruptive venture was about improving the pay and conditions of the players – arguing that the prime motive was 'to force the Australian Cricket Board to sell him the TV rights to their matches'[27] – he nonetheless felt that it had brought forth some useful benefits. At long last the game's rulers had been forced to get to grips with the commercial world via improved deals with sponsors and TV companies, and more parochially the workload imposed on the West Indian Packer players had increased their professionalism. Walcott was not alone in feeling that the members of the squad had also pulled together more closely during their shared World Series adventure. 'It was after Packer that we really bonded as a team', says Holding.[28]

Fortunately, Walcott's position in partial opposition to the rebels did little or no long-term damage to his bond with the players, who realised that he was doing what he had to do. 'The World Series conflict didn't really sully any relationships', says Holding. 'There was no friction per se, and Clyde was more or less doing the bidding of Joey Carew once it all blew up. He was representing the Board, and people knew that.'[29] For his part Walcott felt that 'the arguments between administrators and players did not damage our relationships permanently',[30] adding that 'I continued to get on well with Clive Lloyd and we worked closely together afterwards. It was messy at the time but good came out of it.'[31]

Despite the disruption caused by the World Series, most of the players from the 1975 World Cup win survived into the squad for the 1979 World Cup finals, which took place in England shortly after the Packer armistice had been signed. Containing a new quartet of excellent cricketers who had made their mark in the absence of the Packer rebels – Kallicharran, Faoud Bacchus, Larry Gomes and Malcolm Marshall – the West Indies were again under Walcott's management, and again favourites to win the tournament. As the squad met up in London for the first time, he detected with relief that no coolness existed between the rebels and the new players, and so there was little difficulty in moulding them into a unified outfit. While it turned out that Bacchus, Gomes and Marshall were not selected for any of the cup games, they were, he said 'cheerful and enthusiastic throughout'.[32]

Boasting a stronger and better-balanced team than in 1975, the West Indies won the tournament with greater ease than they had done four years previously, cantering home in the final at Lord's after Richards had posted 138 in their innings of 286 and their opponents, England, had found the total well out of their reach. As a sign that not everything had changed in the wake of Packer, Walcott, with some embarrassment, had found himself having to inform Lloyd that his captain's fee for the tournament had been set at £50 – equivalent to about £320 in 2023 prices. When Lloyd rejected the offer, Walcott was forced to go back to the board, which raised the sum to a hardly less feeble £100.

As the specialist man for tours of the UK, Walcott's next managerial input came when the West Indies visited England in 1980, having only recently returned from the two parts of their 1979–80 tour to Australia and New Zealand. That Australasian trip had been managed by the Trinidadian former Test player Willie Rodriguez, who had overseen a successful 2–0 series win during the first leg in Australia but then had been unable to keep a lid on things during the New Zealand portion of the tour, which had developed into one of the most acrimonious series of all time, and which the West Indies lost 1–0.

Weary after a long period away from home and upset by the standard of local umpiring, which they felt was tainted with racism, Lloyd and the West Indies players allowed their frustration to get the better of them, while Rodriguez, if anything, fuelled the fire with complaints and public pronouncements rather than trying to exercise a restraining influence. After a number of angry incidents, including Colin Croft deliberately running into umpire Fred Goodall and Holding kicking over the stumps in frustration at a turned-down appeal, Rodriguez supported a squad decision to return home early, until, as Walcott said, 'good sense prevailed and the players saw out the tour'.[33]

Rodriguez, who had declined to properly discipline anyone on the tour, was never invited to manage a trip again, and Walcott, clearly unhappy with what he called the 'unsavoury' turn of events in New Zealand, was determined to restore order on the 1980 England tour. He had new disciplinary clauses written into the players' contracts and, with the support of a rather chastened Lloyd, set up a tour committee to monitor on-the-field behaviour. Speaking to the press early on, Walcott nonetheless cautioned the British public not to expect any lessening in competitive spirit. 'People are saying that we will be trying so hard to be good boys that our game will suffer, but that will not be the case', he warned.[34]

With the Barbadian former West Indies batsman Cammie Smith as his assistant manager, Walcott was able to restore his team's focus and equanimity, so that in retrospect the New Zealand tour turned out to be a watershed moment. Thereafter, the West Indies became perennial world beaters, undefeated across an astounding run of 29 Test match series until 1995. Walcott's commitment to restoring order had been the final piece in the jigsaw, turning Lloyd's side into a highly disciplined sporting outfit. In many ways they were a team in his own image – serious, proud and competitive, but – with the fine-tuning he had introduced in 1980 – also capable of playing the game with good sportsmanship, bright nature and fun.

The 1980 England tour, with Marshall, Joel Garner, Roberts, Croft and Holding now settled in the pace attack, delivered a 1–0 win – a margin of victory that would probably have been much wider were it not for four draws in the five-match series that were partly attributable to wet weather. Across the trip Walcott found that Lloyd was now sufficiently matured as a captain to leave him to his own devices on the cricketing side of things.[35] Beyond the boundary Walcott was able to nurture a more relaxed atmos-phere by allowing wives and families to stay in the team hotel, reckoning that this 'made the players more contented'[36] and helped them to perform better. Members of the squad were also able to use a fleet of sponsored cars that allowed them a bit more flexi-bility as they travelled around the country, although Walcott generally insisted on the tour bus wherever possible, chiefly for the camaraderie and team spirit it engendered.

Though successful, the tour was not without problems for the manager to wrestle with. Chief of these was a decision by Greenidge to serialise parts of his autobiography in the *Sun* newspaper, which focused on passages that criticised his teammates and captain Lloyd, of whom he said: 'I do not think Clive will go down in history as one of the game's inspirational captains'.[37] Walcott was deeply unimpressed by the lurid headlines, and Greenidge ended up trying to get the book withdrawn from British shops. Although the issue was dealt with internally, it created temporary tensions between Greenidge, whom Walcott described as 'something of a loner',[38] and the rest of the squad.

In the final Test at Old Trafford, Walcott also had to deliver a rallying cry to Lloyd, who tore a hamstring during the rain-affected match and was forced to pass the captaincy over, temporarily, to Richards. 'Clive was so downhearted about it that he talked about retiring and handing over to Viv', he said.[39] 'I told him not even to think about it.'[40] Nonetheless, it was from that point onwards that Richards began to become impatient for a handover of the captaincy, later talking about a 'conspiracy' to deprive him from taking over the leadership – a suggestion that Walcott firmly rejected.

Though Walcott's chief contributions as a manager came mainly on tours to England, where he was regarded as the proven specialist, he also took on less onerous administrative duties during home Test series, which he could fit in more amenably with his full-time work at Barbados Shipping and Trading. When England visited the Caribbean for the 1980–81 tour of the West Indies, his managerial and diplomatic skills were again in demand, this time to help find a solution to an external, rather than internal, difficulty.

The second Test of the five-match series was due to be held in Georgetown on 28 February 1981, but two days before the game the Guyanese prime minister, Forbes Burnham, a hardline opponent of apartheid, announced that his government would be deporting the 35-year-old England player Robin Jackman, who had been flown out as a replacement for the injured Bob Willis. Burnham objected to Jackman on the grounds that he had spent several winters playing cricket in South Africa, and argued that under the 1977 Gleneagles Agreement, which forbade contacts between members of the Commonwealth and South Africa, he should not be allowed into the country. England, on the principle that their team selection should not be dictated by the views of a foreign government, announced that they would be withdrawing from the Test, immediately putting the whole tour in jeopardy.

Walcott's opposition to apartheid was in many ways as staunch as that of Burnham – indeed Michael Manley described him as 'one of the strongest and most outspoken advocates of the isolation of South Africa'[41] – but he felt that Guyana's prime minister was grandstanding, and that his stance was not one supported by the majority of people in the Caribbean. So when the England tour manager, Alan Smith, rang him to see if his squad and entourage might be allowed to come to Barbados as a place of refuge, he was happy to offer his diplomatic services to try to keep the tour on track.

Having rung the prime minister of Barbados, Tom Adams, Walcott was able not only to persuade him to allow England to make their base on the island but to agree to an emergency meeting between representatives of the governments of Barbados, Antigua, Montserrat and Jamaica to decide on how to move matters forward.

'It's no exaggeration to say that the whole tour was up in the air',[42] says Reds Perreira, who was sporting director of the Organisation of Eastern Caribbean States at the time. 'If other Caribbean nations had taken the same view as Guyana, then the whole thing would have been off – it was very worrying. We were trying to get a consensus among the prime ministers, and Clyde, given the status and respect he commanded, was key to that. He played a leading role in a very crucial situation.'[43]

After lengthy talks involving Walcott, on 3 March 1981 the heads of government announced that they had agreed to allow England to continue with the last three scheduled Tests of the tour in Barbados, Antigua and Jamaica, and that their interpretation of the Gleneagles Agreement meant they would not be stepping in the way of Jackman playing, if selected. In the event, he appeared in two of the Tests, with limited impact, and the West Indies won the series 2–0.

The rest of the tour was tinged with sadness at the death of England's assistant manager, Ken Barrington, who had a heart attack in the team hotel on the second evening of the Barbados Test. Walcott and Muriel had invited Barrington and his wife, Anne, to dine with them at their home in Bridgetown that night, but the offer had been regretfully declined because of a prior engagement. Walcott felt the stress of the Jackman affair may have had some bearing on his friend's death, observing that the machinations in Guyana 'caused him a lot of anguish'.[44]

Apartheid again embroiled Walcott in controversy less than two years later, when 16 West Indies players signed up for a rebel tour of South Africa, organised in defiance of the worldwide ban on cricketing relations with that country that had stood since 1970. Led by the Jamaican batsman Lawrence Rowe, most of the rebels were fringe members of the West Indies set-up, either not yet established in the team or on their way out – although there were also players of the calibre of Colin Croft, Alvin Kallicharran and Sylvester Clarke, who could have been expected to play many Tests for the official West Indies side in the future.

Renegade tours by English and Sri Lankan players had taken place over the previous two years, but the idea that cricketers from the Caribbean might follow suit was thought highly unlikely, despite the huge amounts of money on offer. Recruitment of the West Indies rebels had been organised under the tightest levels of secrecy by the South African authorities, and the world's press had no inkling that anything of the kind was under way – until Walcott provided the tip-off that blew their cover.

He gave his scoop to Reds Perreira, who was living in Barbados at the time and working as a cricket commentator. On 11 January 1983 Perreira was making his way by car to Kensington Oval, and as his vehicle paused at a pedestrian crossing, Walcott suddenly emerged by his window, leaning in to whisper: 'There's a rebel team going to South Africa. Do your homework',[45] before disappearing as quickly as he had arrived.

For Perreira it was the news lead of a lifetime. After making contact with a source at British West Indian Airways (BWIA) to see if there were any noteworthy passengers in the forthcoming schedules, he discovered that eight first-class Bajan cricketers were booked in to fly to Miami the following day, and on the basis of that information he broke the story to the world at lunchtime, without naming names.

'Just about everybody came to the airport the next day, and my reputation was at stake', he says.

> None of the players were on the BWIA flight and I was beginning to sweat, but then a porter told me he had seen one of the rebels, Alvin Greenidge, with his suitcase, and suddenly there was a bus screaming into the airport with the rest of them. They had used BWIA as a decoy and were travelling by American Airlines. I was a relieved man, I can tell you, but it was thanks to Clyde Walcott that I got the story. I've never told anyone that before – but it was him.[46]

Quite how Walcott got wind of the rebels' imminent departure is unclear, and afterwards he declined to expand on his cryptic message to Perreira. But it is likely that he learned something from one of the West Indies players who had been approached by South Africa but had turned down the offer. As Barbados is a small island and Walcott was a man with many contacts, he would have been in an excellent position to keep abreast of developments, even if they were cloaked in secrecy.

Walcott was appalled by the actions of the rebels, which he thought 'brought no credit to anyone',[47] and fully backed the lifetime bans they were subsequently handed by the West Indies Board. 'I could not support any black man going to South Africa and being classed as an "honorary white"', he said.[48] 'That was repugnant and dishonourable.'[49]

With one or two exceptions, the rebels were hardly missed by the main West Indies side, and Walcott's deliberations over selection were barely impinged upon as a result of their bans. Later that year, in 1983, only Kallicharran and Croft might have strengthened the side that took part in the third World Cup.

That tournament was again staged in England, but in a surprise move the West Indies managerial role was handed to the West Indies Board's Guyanese chief executive, Steve Camacho (1945–2015), rather than to Walcott. 'We won the 1975 tournament, and the one in 1979, and I think we might well have made it a hat trick in 1983 had I remained in charge for a third time', said Walcott.[50] 'Steve ... was a protégé of mine and a long-time friend, [so] I had no criticism of their decision. But I was expecting to be manager in 1983 ... [and] I felt that the team would have benefited from the continuity of having Clive Lloyd and me once again.'[51] Although the West Indies managed to get to the final at Lord's, they were beaten unexpectedly by India after trying to chase a small total of 183 with reckless abandon, rather than quietly compiling the necessary runs in the many overs available to them. 'I was frantic, wanting to go into the dressing room to tell them to hold back, but I decided against it', Walcott said.[52]

It was unfortunate that Walcott was deprived of one last World Cup hurrah with Lloyd, as the following year, at the age of 39, Lloyd retired from Test cricket, leaving Richards to move into the leadership role.

Walcott was back as manager for the 1987 World Cup, which was held in India and Pakistan. By then, although Richards had carried on Lloyd's formidable winning record as captain, the West Indies were beginning to take on a slightly less formidable hue, and their fast-bowling resources were reduced to Patrick Patterson, Courtney Walsh and Winston Benjamin. Walcott tried to persuade Joel Garner to postpone his retirement for the World Cup, but he refused, and as a consequence the side was forced to rely too heavily on back-up support with the ball from Roger Harper, Carl

Hooper and Richards himself. Failing to make it to the knockout stage after two defeats against England and one against Pakistan, a frustrated Walcott finally lost his 100 per cent success rate as a World Cup manager.

In 1988, having spent two decades in the service of the West Indies Cricket Board of Control, Walcott was finally appointed as its first black president, simultaneously relinquishing his role as a selector. 'It has often been remarked that it took three decades of Test cricket before a black captain was given permanent tenure of the West Indies team [but just] as remarkably, it took nearly another three before a black president was elected by the Board', points out the cricket author David Woodhouse.[53] Some of the ten presidents of the board who came before Walcott, including his immediate predecessor, the Jamaican Allan Rae, had traces of mixed blood, but since its formation in the early 1920s all of its leaders had been what Woodhouse characterised as 'census white'.[54]

The appointment of a black head of West Indies cricket for the next five years was an especially welcome development for captain Richards, who as much as any player over the previous decade had publicly signalled the importance of a racially conscious approach to his game. While Walcott's relationship with Richards was perhaps not as easy as it had been with Lloyd, they forged an alliance over the next three years of his presidency that allowed for a continuation of the previous decade of success.

Richards was one of Walcott's favourite players – hardly surprising given the similarities in their dominant batting styles – and the two of them shared a fierce will to win. 'As the successor to Clive Lloyd as captain he led by example and did a good job', said Walcott.[55] 'Viv always had a smile and was easy-going. But he hated losing and would sometimes get worked up if he didn't think enough was being done to stop the opposition coming out on top. He had one or two scrapes off the field and there were occasions when I had to cover for him.'[56]

One of those came in 1990, after the captain crossed swords during a Test match against England in Antigua with the *Daily Express* journalist James Lawton, who had written a critical story about him the day before. Instead of taking to the field with the rest of the team at the start of play, Richards stormed up to the press box to remonstrate with Lawton, and was absent when the first ball of the session was bowled. 'It was a major error of judgement on his part',[57] said Walcott, who sought, and received, an apology from Richards to the board and the team. He also required a contrite letter from Richards the following year when the skipper had a heated row with Bobby Simpson, the coach on Australia's 1991 tour to the Caribbean. 'Some of my colleagues on the Board wanted tougher action, but I persuaded them that an apology was sufficient', he revealed later.[58]

Walcott and Richards maintained their good relationship right up to the end of Richards's career in

August 1991, when after his 121st Test appearance and his 50th as captain at the age of 39, he was quoted as saying that he was retiring as skipper – and waved in valedictory fashion to the Oval crowd in London at the end of his second innings during the final Test against England.

Moving into personnel manager mode, Walcott seized on the moment by asking Richards to put his decision in writing, so that a succession plan could be swiftly developed. Richards subsequently appears to have felt the matter was conducted with undue haste, and that he had not in any case made a definitive decision to retire before being bustled out of the door. 'He seemed to blame me for contributing to his retirement', conceded Walcott later.[59] '[But] with the World Cup coming up we had to be looking to the future. He didn't tell me he wanted to carry on, and Richie Richardson was appointed to lead the side.'[60] Although his relationship with Richards survived that rather abrupt ending, it was a slightly sour note on which to finish a successful partnership.

Walcott served as West Indies Board president for a further two years after Richard's departure, and in office was able to extend an invitation to South Africa to rejoin the cricketing fold in the wake of the release of Nelson Mandela in 1990.

Tenacious of the opinion that there could be no rapprochement with South Africa until apartheid was completely ended, Walcott had for many years been suspicious that the predominantly white cricketing boards would have done a deal with the regime if at all possible. 'That would have split the cricket world into two: [with] the white countries ... playing among themselves and the non-white countries ... doing the same thing', he argued.[61] 'That would have been a tragedy of the highest magnitude [but] thankfully it never happened.'[62]

In 1988, shortly after taking up the presidency of the West Indies Board, Walcott had represented the region at the ICC when the subject of easing the restrictions on South Africa was discussed at great length. Although a resumption of Test cricket was not on the agenda at that point, some ICC member countries felt that cricketers should be able to play in South Africa if they wanted to, and that to continue to prevent them from doing so was a restraint of trade. Walcott, bolstered by the firm personal support of various Caribbean political leaders, led a rearguard action to prevent anything of the kind from happening.

By 1991, however, the dismantling of apartheid had progressed at such a pace that both Walcott and the West Indies Board were at last prepared to sanction a change in direction. As a result, the ICC was able to reinstate South Africa as a Test-playing nation, although not without a slight delay when Walcott, feeling the process was being rushed without proper consideration, abstained during the crucial vote. Symbolically, and at Walcott's invitation, the first

Test match after re-admission took place on Walcott's home ground against the West Indies in Bridgetown, Barbados, in April 1992, part of a three-match series which the home side, under Richardson, won 1–0.

By then, Walcott's statesman-like skills at the ICC on behalf of the West Indies Board had won him admirers across the nine member countries, and in 1993 he was appointed as the first non-British, non-white chairman of the organisation, ushering in an era of change that began to focus the attention of international cricket away from its traditional base at Lord's and towards the other powerhouses of the game. At the time the West Indies Board was one such powerhouse, occupying a short-lived position of moral and political eminence that was quickly lost due to its lack of financial muscle, with a consequent deterioration in terms of cricketing expertise and administrative competence.

Walcott's ICC appointment, which required him to stand down from the presidency of the West Indies Board, was the culmination of a quarter century of hard work in cricket administration that had taken him from a relatively humble position on the Guyanese board to the most important post in cricket in his region and then to the highest position in world cricket.

Over that period the West Indies had become a dominant playing force in the game – arguably the most commanding in history, with a golden period from February 1981 to December 1989 in which they won 40 of their 69 Tests and lost just seven. Helped immeasurably by their players' access to English county cricket, which provided them with financial rewards as well as a great technical grounding, they were magnificent across the years of Walcott's presidency, and even after the departure of Lloyd and Richards were able to maintain a proud record under Richardson, despite finding themselves less well provided for in terms of playing resources.

As Manley has pointed out, the raised status of West Indies cricket helped Walcott to gain his post at the top of the ICC, for 'no matter how appropriate his appointment might have been, it would not have occurred to anyone even to propose him if the West Indies had not become an immense, if not the dominant, force in the modern game'.[63] Of course, Walcott was only one of a number of influential figures who had helped the West Indies to their position of superiority. But unlike many others, he was omnipresent; a consistently significant force across the years whose ethos and sensibilities contributed greatly to the West Indies' remarkable journey towards ascendancy. Now he was ready to make his influence felt upon a wider stage.

# 7

# ICC and beyond

Walcott's appointment as chairman of the ICC was a ground-breaking development that sparked a wholesale modernisation of an organisation that had remained largely unchanged in outlook since its formation in 1909 as the Imperial Cricket Conference.

The governing body of world cricket, it had initially consisted only of representatives from England, Australia and South Africa, but had admitted the West Indies, New Zealand and India in 1926, Pakistan in 1947, Sri Lanka in 1981 and Zimbabwe in 1992. Various associate members, including the Netherlands and Bermuda, had also been added over the years, so that by the time Walcott took up his post in July 1993 the ICC – now renamed the International Cricket Council – had become a truly global body with many successes in terms of spreading the game across the world.

Nonetheless, it was still steeped in traditions and archaic practices. From its inception the ICC had been hosted and administered at Lord's by the MCC, an exclusive private members' club whose president had automatically become chairman of the ICC. Only when Walcott's predecessor, Colin Cowdrey, was given the post in 1989 was this precedent broken. Although Cowdrey was still English, his arrival had at least set in train a period of reform that Walcott was able to continue to oversee.

Pressure for that reform had been accelerated by Walcott himself, when, as president of the West Indies Board he had persuaded his former schoolfriend Eric Bishop, a retired judge in Barbados, to come up with proposals for change. The resulting document led to a seven-page West Indies resolution at the ICC's 1992 summer meeting which called, among other things, for an end to the traditional veto held by England and Australia over all ICC decisions. Walcott's lobbying in that direction, allied to the clear, principled positions he had taken on South Africa, earned him much credit among the more progressive elements of cricket's administrative circles, helping to stoke the quiet campaign to insert him as ICC chairman.

Having served as an ICC match referee in three England v. Pakistan Tests in 1992, fining Rashid Latif for serious dissent and handing wicketkeeper Moin Khan a dressing down for frenzied appealing, he also brought much benefit to his cause when the ICC sat down, in 1992, to debate the venue for the 1996 World Cup. Alan Smith, one of England's representatives during that long, wearying discussion in London, described it as 'the most acrimonious meeting I have ever attended',[1] and it was in no small part due to Walcott's diplomatic skills that it did not break up in complete disarray. Although the encounter was chaired by Cowdrey, it was Walcott who played the key role in breaking the angry deadlock, thrashing out a compromise that allowed India, Pakistan and Sri Lanka to jointly host the finals at the expense of England, who agreed to step aside in exchange for the right to stage the 1999 World Cup. 'I think that my work background of industrial relations with unions helped', he said afterwards. 'When I left that meeting I felt I had a great chance of being ICC chairman.'[2]

There was also a lengthy and inconclusive debate in 1992 on abolishing England and Australia's ICC veto, and it was only the following year, when Walcott was able to put his full weight behind the proposal as chairman, that it was voted through. Once in office he presided over a number of other changes, most notably via votes in his first year to put an end to the MCC's ability to appoint the chairman, while simultaneously taking away its administrative role in ICC affairs. Although Lord's would continue to be the ICC's base, henceforth it would have its own newly appointed full-time chief executive, an Australian, David Richards, supported by a small number of employees and with Walcott continuing to oversee operations as its unpaid figurehead, chairing the executive board of member representatives.

The following year the ICC established a commercial wing directed by a development committee under
the chairmanship of the South African Ali Bacher – a
key development given its need to increase returns
from the main source of its income, the World Cup.
Walcott also oversaw a move towards more flexibility
in the body's decision-making, reducing its previously
cumbersome reliance on an annual conference in
London by introducing teleconferences and increasing
the frequency of executive committee meetings.

In the process, Walcott's chairmanship helped to trans-
form the ICC from a stodgy debating chamber into an
increasingly decisive and fleet-footed organisation that
could more efficiently focus on its role in developing,
coordinating, regulating and promoting cricket worldwide. With control of the game's direction and administration wrested from the MCC, plus a new regime that
made its decisions binding on all members, the ICC's
paramountcy at last became clear and undisputed. With
Walcott at its head – a black man from outside the traditional power bases of England and Australia – no one
could deny that times were a-changing. 'Once a bastion
of traditional values with all the good and the bad things
the term implies, cricket was now responding to the
currents of change throughout the world, and Walcott's
appointment reflected the new dynamics', concluded
Michael Manley.[3]

That is not to say that the new chairman swept
all before him in a frenzy of radical reform. Although

Walcott felt that the MCC had 'controlled cricket in an imperial sort of way'[4] that was 'not good for the game',[5] as a figure who deeply appreciated the traditions of cricket he was not about to challenge any of its long-held tenets. On the other hand, he was certainly keen on shifting influence into new areas, and on giving the hitherto overlooked Test playing nations – the West Indies, India, Pakistan, Zimbabwe and Sri Lanka – a greater say in the future of the game.

It was partly as a result of the Walcott-led reforms that India subsequently became a much more influential force in cricket administration and that, within a couple of years of Walcott's arrival, the Indian cricket administrator and businessman Jagmohan Dalmiya had emerged as a leading contender to succeed Walcott in his post. In the new spirit of democracy, future ICC leaders were now required to be elected by a two-thirds majority rather than appointed, and after some machinations Dalmiya was eventually voted in as successor to Walcott.

Beginning what had now become a fixed three-year term of office in July 1997, Dalmiya's title was altered to president, though the post was essentially the same. At the same time, by popular demand, Walcott was appointed to a new, unpaid, role of chairman of the ICC's cricket committee, responsible, among other things, for maintaining standards of player behaviour, appointing and assessing umpires and referees, and general management of the game. With Dalmiya's

natural priorities focused on developing the commercial side of international cricket – never a strong suit
for Walcott, who had more interest in the playing side
of the game – the division of responsibilities was good
for both men.

Under his reign as ICC chairman Walcott had
already been involved in bringing forward fresh ways
of thinking that presaged his new duties as chairman of
the cricket committee – including the introduction of
third umpires and TV replays and the acceptance
of the Duckworth-Lewis method to adjust run targets
in rain-affected one-day internationals. Now his focus
would be on building a behavioural framework for
global cricket.

Chief weapon in that mission was the ICC's Code
of Conduct, introduced in 1992, which set out how
players were expected to approach the game in terms
of discipline, honesty and sportsmanship – all areas
close to Walcott's heart. Over the next three years he
spent much of his time trying to find solutions to
thorny issues such as ball tampering, suspect bowling
actions, intimidatory bowling, match fixing, sledging
and excessive appealing. On the excessive use of
short bowling he was able to lobby successfully for
an allowance of two bouncers an over rather than
one, having crossed swords with the ICC over that
'absolutely ridiculous' restriction in the past. He also
helped to bring into being a more permanent team of
Test match referees, allowing umpires to concentrate

on their core duties while the referees could take a harder line on sledging, bad language and appealing.

On the other hand, Walcott was able to make much less progress on tackling bribery and match-fixing allegations, partly due to difficulties in gathering watertight evidence but also because member countries, rather than the ICC itself, were at the time responsible for investigating such matters. By the time he stepped down as chairman of the cricket committee in 2000, at the age of 74, he had still not been able fully to get to grips with the situation.

Despite that frustration, Walcott's time as cricket committee chairman was a successful one, as was his period from 1993 to 1997 as overall head of the ICC. Perhaps the only failure that could be laid at his door during his seven years of service was an inability during the 1996 World Cup to find a compromise when the Australia and West Indies squads refused to play their scheduled fixtures in Sri Lanka due to fears about the Tamil Tigers terrorist group's activities there. Despite his best efforts, Walcott was unable to persuade either team to change their mind, describing the tempestuous key meeting between the various parties as the most difficult he had ever had to chair at the ICC. In the end both teams had to forfeit their points. Walcott's only consolation was that Sri Lanka, with whom he had much sympathy over the issue, went on to win the competition by playing a new brand of aggressive pinch-hitting cricket that captivated the competition's global audience and was much in keeping with Walcott's batting philosophy.

Even if Walcott had gone on to achieve little as head of the ICC, his appointment would have been important in itself – a signal that the old ways were no longer the best ways. The fact that his tenure was marked by significant change and solid accomplishment made it even more notable. In this way there were parallels between Walcott's move into the ICC chairmanship and Worrell's earlier ascendency to the West Indies captaincy: both were long-awaited symbolic moments, yet were also followed by tangible, widely acclaimed progress and a notable change in outlook. Ivo Tennant noted that Worrell's achievements as captain not only showed 'that a black man could be as good a leader – and in his case a better leader – than the white men who had gone before' but 'expanded the conception of West Indians and cultivated the image of the black man around the world'.[6] So it was with Walcott at the ICC.

Whether Walcott's breath of fresh air ushered in a better era for cricket is a matter for debate, given that the adjustments he helped to introduce opened up the field to a set of future administrators – both at the ICC and on the boards of each cricketing nation – whose backgrounds were more aligned to accountancy than to cricket. Walcott accepted this as the possible price of change, but also recognised the dangers. 'There has to be a balance between those ex-cricketers like myself who want to serve in order to put something back into the game and those without a cricketing background who join the various boards to offer their financial and commercial expertise', he said.[7] Unfortunately, in this wish he would have been disappointed, as Walcott turned out to be one of the last of his kind: the unpaid former player with a significant say in how the international game is run.

For Walcott, departure from the ICC in 2000 was, in effect, a departure from cricket. Although he subsequently accepted occasional minor ambassadorial duties on his home island while also staying in contact with the West Indies Board as an informal adviser, he settled down to the quiet life of full retirement in Bridgetown with Muriel. Towards the end of his time at the ICC, and knowing that his days at the epicentre of the game were drawing to a close, he had written a second autobiography, *Sixty Years on the Back Foot*, which was published in 1999 as an update to his original 1958 memoirs, *Island Cricketers*, and which served as his final reflections on a remarkable career.

Over the years Walcott's work had brought him a number of honours. In 1966 he was awarded an OBE by the British government, and on his departure from Guyana in 1970 the administration there honoured him with its Golden Arrow of Achievement. In 1991 he received the Gold Crown of Merit (Barbados) and in 1993 he was made a Knight of St Andrew, Order of Barbados, giving him the title Sir Clyde Walcott. The second of the three Ws to be knighted (Worrell's came in 1964 and Weekes had his in 1995), he was invited to London to have the honour bestowed upon him by Queen Elizabeth II, but decided instead to stay at home to receive his award from Dame Nita Barrow, the governor-general of Barbados and sister of Errol Barrow, who had guided the country to independence as its first prime minister. It was a typically independent Walcottian gesture, delivered without fuss or offence but with just the right amount of quiet conviction to make his point.

During the last few years of Walcott's life in Barbados, the spirit remained but the health began to fail, and in the later stages he was cared for devotedly at home by Muriel, who had always been a strong and supportive influence while ploughing her own furrow in Guyana and Barbados as a teacher, librarian, personnel officer and business manager. He died after a short illness at the Queen Elizabeth Hospital in Bridgetown, not far from his home, on 26 August 2006, with his family at his side. He was 80.

There was a genuine, worldwide outpouring of sadness at Walcott's death. 'He was not only one of the greatest-ever post-war cricketers but also one of the finest people I have ever had the opportunity of working with',[8] said the Pakistani cricket administrator Ehsan Mani, who later became head of the ICC himself. 'He was a gentle but decisive man for whom cricket always came first and his own ego last',[9] said the Australian administrator Malcolm Gray, while for Gerald Majola, CEO of Cricket South Africa, he was 'a fierce opponent of apartheid in sport [who was] instrumental in changing the face of West Indies cricket and helped to revolutionise world cricket, which had [previously] been very much a colonial sport'.[10] Everton Weekes called him 'a true friend and a great man',[11] and Lance Gibbs remembered him as 'one of our greatest ambassadors ... a dominant individual [who] will be a great loss indeed'.[12]

Walcott's funeral took place on 2 September 2006 at St Mary's Anglican Church in Bridgetown, which was bursting to the seams with more than 500 people, including the former West Indies captains Garfield Sobers and Brian Lara. His body, wearing a West Indies team tie inside a coffin draped with a West Indies Cricket Board flag, was later taken for burial on a hill overlooking the eastern end of the Three Ws Oval cricket ground at the centre of the Cave Hill campus of the University of West Indies. The ground had been named in honour of Walcott, Worrell and Weekes, and was already the resting place of Worrell, who had died of leukaemia at the early age of 42 in 1967. When Weekes passed away in 2020, 20 years after Walcott and at the age of 95, the three were finally reunited there – and commemorated nearby with an imposing 3Ws monument bearing the busts of each of them.

Two months after Walcott's burial in Barbados, a service of thanksgiving for his life was held in London at St John's Wood Church, next to Lord's. Muriel and Michael were in attendance, along with a host of admirers from the cricketing world, and there were tributes from, among others, the MCC president Doug Insole and a former Enfield teammate, Edward Slinger.

Muriel died more than a decade later, in 2019, at the age of 92. Asked once which of the three Ws had been her favourite cricketer, she confided, impishly, that it was Worrell, whom she had greatly admired for his stylish batting, which she described as 'poetry in motion'.[13]

It was typical of Worrell that he could steal the limelight even in Walcott's own household, but it would never have worried Muriel's husband, who had achieved so much in cricket, and life, that there was no need for insecurity. Worrell was undoubtedly a great man and a great agent of change, but Walcott was every bit his equal.

# 8

# An assessment

Comparing Clyde Walcott with Frank Worrell might seem an unnecessary exercise, yet it is worth considering that while Worrell is widely regarded as a black icon, Walcott does not quite command the same profile.

This is puzzling in some ways, understandable in others. Worrell was a charismatic personality whose rise to the captaincy of the West Indies coincided with an intense period of Caribbean – indeed worldwide – agitation against colonialism that led to independence in many states shortly after his appointment. Worrell's elevation was a symbolic moment in that long nationalist struggle, and he embraced the bright new dawn of black leadership in the best possible way – mixing statesmanlike gravitas with an exhilarating commitment to the enjoyment of cricket for its own sake. Later, through his work in academia at the University of the West Indies and in politics within the Jamaican senate, he showed a seriousness of purpose that sat well with those who argued that black attainment should not just be measured in terms of sport and the arts.

Walcott, by contrast, was a lower-key individual, rather more conservative in outlook and demeanour, less easy to latch onto as an inspiring personality in the realm of black consciousness. Although he was a prominent character in the early 1950s when the body of non-white West Indies players strove to assert their rights – and for a time in the late 1950s was as close to attaining the captaincy as anyone – it was Worrell who emerged into the global limelight as the first permanent black leader of the team. Subsequently, Walcott's contribution to the black cause was confined mainly to cricket, but was arguably more substantial and, thanks in part to Worrell's early death, more sustained. Yet the work he carried out was nearly always of a backroom nature – behind the scenes and more likely to go unheralded. Thus it was that Worrell became the hero during Walcott's playing years, and that Clive Lloyd and Viv Richards took the plaudits in the glorious years of West Indies dominance.

Walcott would not have complained about this – indeed he never did. But it seems unfair that he did not receive more acclaim for what he achieved. He was a major catalyst for change on and off the cricket field, and a man who gave huge input to the cause of black nationalism as well as the game, and society more generally.

His first sphere of influence was, of course, as a cricketer, something at which he was, quite simply, brilliant. One of the most successful batsmen of all time, along with Worrell and Weekes he became the first of the Barbados greats, and a catalyst for that island's extraordinarily outsized contribution to the world of cricket. Before Walcott's arrival, Barbados had served up a number of notable players to the West Indies side, but none of an exceptional order. Afterwards it fully established itself as the strong centre of cricket we know today, providing players of the calibre of Garfield Sobers, Hall and Griffith, Seymour Nurse, Conrad Hunte, Malcolm Marshall, Joel Garner, Greenidge and Haynes. Of all the contributory factors behind this sporting miracle, the inspiration of Walcott must be one of the most important.

Having scored an average of more than 56 runs every time he played a Test innings – and with only George Headley, Weekes and Sobers averaging higher among West Indies batsmen – Walcott remains one of the top 20 highest averaging batsmen of all time, above the likes of Len Hutton, Sachin Tendulkar, Brian Lara, Len Hutton and Viv Richards in the pecking order. In the regularly updated ICC all-time rankings – which take into account match situations and the standard of bowling – he is consistently positioned in the top ten, level on points with Sobers, Richards and Kumar Sangakkara, and comfortably ahead of the other two Ws.

For Barbados, British Guiana and Enfield, Walcott was a focal point of consistent excellence, driving each team forward with his raw power. But it was with the West Indies that he made his greatest impact, not just in terms of the runs he scored but in the way he compiled them. During an era of West Indian foment, Walcott's hard-hitting, awe-inspiring batsmanship was greeted with glee across the Caribbean as a proud, uncompromising statement of independence, free from the strictures of the game as imagined by other nations and fully in line with the template laid down by the fathers of West Indies cricket, Learie Constantine and George Headley – a West Indian style of play that was feisty and free-spirited, yet with a disciplined core.

As Simon Lister has said, 'Walcott was scoring his runs for a nation; those runs belonged to the people, and the people knew it.'[1] In a region where cricket exerted a symbolic influence reaching well beyond the boundary, the age of the three Ws, during which Walcott was the best batsman in the world in the mid-1950s, transformed the West Indies into a serious cricketing force and in so doing bolstered the nationalist cause across the region. Walcott played his part, too, in the internal struggles of West Indies cricket – fights that reflected the external battles to wrestle power from a white minority across the Caribbean. As an ally of Weekes and Worrell, who both had strong claims to the captaincy, and as a man who had a convincing leadership case himself, Walcott did as much as anyone to push for change in that direction. While in the end the pressure of that tussle led to his early retirement from the game, it did at least help to pave the way for Worrell to become captain in 1960.

In administration, Walcott's contribution to West Indies cricket was, if anything, even more significant. His cricket organiser role in British Guiana revitalised the colony's fortunes in the regional game, while helping to develop an array of brilliant new Guyanese players who became the backbone of West Indies success for years to come. Simultaneously, he stimulated new self-worth and a more tangible Caribbean identity among the Indian population of the sugar estates on which he worked. In his subsequent position as a social welfare organiser on those plantations, he also did much to enhance living and working conditions as part of the Sugar Producers Association's long-running programme of improvements.

Moving from his Guyanese adventures into business in Barbados, where he was a ground-breaking black figure in various positions, his voluntary work for the West Indies Board, including as selector, manager and its first black president, established him as the most reliable, consistent administrative presence over the most successful era in West Indies' Test history. He also led the West Indies' combative line on what he called the 'savage tyranny'[2] of apartheid, maintaining steadfast opposition to any backsliding on South Africa's exile during a period when many members of the international cricketing establishment would have brought the country back into the fold at the slightest excuse.

By turning to global cricket administration as the ICC's first non-white chairman, Walcott's role in modernising that global body's infrastructure and outlook was far-reaching, transforming it into a more powerful and influential organisation that much better represented the international community of cricket. It is perhaps no coincidence that after Walcott left the West Indies Board and the ICC, the respect in which both organisations were held began to wane. No figure of such genuine stature has held the most powerful jobs in those two bodies since he exited.

Walcott, then, was a powerhouse both on and off the field, one of the dominant personalities of international cricket across five decades, and a man whose influence also went well beyond the game. No other single individual, both as a player and an administrator, has done more to help West Indies cricket, and few have made a bigger impact on cricket in general.

More than that, he went about his work in a fashion that was universally admired and praised for its humanity and wisdom. 'He was one of the big men of cricket', said the journalist Brian Scovell, who got to know Walcott by helping him to write *Sixty Years on the Back Foot*. 'Not only did he tower over his fellow players and administrators, he brought decency and fair play to the game he loved.'[3] Michael Manley saw him as 'a big man of considerable intelligence and immense innate dignity' who was 'fully deserving of the highest position[s] in international cricket because of his qualities'.[4] Ian McDonald remembered him as 'a very fine man – intelligent, companionable and forceful when necessary',[5] while Jack Simmons recalls him simply as 'one of the nicest people I've ever met'.[6]

Throughout his time as a player, welfare organiser and administrator, Walcott's long-serving dedication to his various causes – most of which went unpaid – stretched far beyond anything that might have been expected of him. Although he maintained that 'I can never do more for cricket than cricket has done for me',[7] any totting up of a notional balance sheet would certainly show the game in substantial arrears. In any form of social accounting, too, Walcott's work to advance racial and societal equity would place many in his debt.

# Timeline

1926:   Born in Bridgetown, Barbados

1938:   Makes debut in Barbados league for Combermere School

1942:   First-class debut for Barbados, aged 16

1944:   Joins Spartan CC in Barbados

1946:   Makes his highest first-class score of 314 not out for Barbados v. Trinidad in Port of Spain, putting on a partnership of 574 with Frank Worrell

1948:   Appears in his Test debut for the West Indies, against England in Bridgetown, aged 21

1950:   Scores 168 not out in the 2nd Test at Lord's to help the West Indies to their first Test victory in England

1951:   Marries Muriel Ashby in Barbados

1951:   Gives up wicketkeeping to focus on batting

1951:   Joins Enfield CC in the Lancashire League, playing for them in English summers until 1954

1954:   Scores 698 runs in home series against England, including his highest Test innings of 220, averaging 87.25

1954:   Moves to British Guiana to become cricket organiser for the Sugar Producers' Association

1955:   Makes debut for British Guiana against his old team Barbados

1955:   Compiles five centuries at home against Australia, scoring the most runs ever in a Test series in the West Indies – 827 at an average of 82.70

1956:   Becomes captain of British Guiana, leading them to three regional titles

1957:   Appointed West Indies vice-captain for tour to England

1958:   Chosen as a Wisden Cricketer of the Year

1958:   Announces retirement from Test cricket, aged 32

1958:   Autobiographical book, *Island Cricketers*, published in the UK

1960:   Comes briefly out of retirement to play two final Test matches, against England at home

1961:   Appointed social welfare organiser by the Sugar Producers' Association in British Guiana

1964:   Plays his last game for British Guiana and retires from first-class cricket, aged 38

1966:   Awarded OBE by the UK government

1968: Becomes president of the Guyana Cricket
Board of Control, holding the post until 1970
1969: Appointed manager of the West Indies tour to
England
1970: Awarded the Golden Arrow of Achievement
by the Guyanese government
1970: Resigns from his work in Guyana and returns
to his homeland to become personnel officer
at Barbados Shipping and Trading, rising to
be chief personnel officer and an executive
director
1972: Becomes vice-president of the Barbados
Cricket Association, serving until 1987
1973: Management duties with the West Indies
during their home series against Australia
1975: The West Indies win the World Cup with
Walcott as manager
1976: Manager of the West Indies tour to England
1978: Elected president of the Barbados Employers'
Federation, remaining in office until 1981
1979: The West Indies win the World Cup for a
second time under Walcott's managership
1987: Manager of the West Indies in the World Cup;
team knocked out at the group stage
1988: Becomes president of the West Indies Cricket
Board, remaining in post until 1993
1990: Takes retirement from his position at
Barbados Shipping and Trading

## Timeline

1991: Awarded the Barbados Gold Crown of Merit
1992: Referees three matches for the International
       Cricket Council
1993: Becomes chairman of the International
       Cricket Council, serving until 1997
1993: Created a Knight of St Andrew in the Order of
       Barbados, with the title Sir Clyde Walcott
1997: Becomes chairman of the International
       Cricket Council's cricket committee, holding
       the post until 2000
1999: Second autobiography, *Sixty Years on the
       Back Foot*, is published
2006: Dies in Barbados, aged 80
2019: Muriel dies in Barbados, aged 92

# Statistics

## Statistical record

*Information supplied by The Association of Cricket Statisticians and Historians*

### First-class record (batting and fielding)

| Year | M | I | NO | Runs | HS | Ave | 100 | 50 | ct | st |
|------|---|---|----|----|----|-----|-----|----|----|----|
| 1941–2 | 1 | 2 | 0 | 8 | 8 | 4.00 | – | – | – | – |
| 1942 | 2 | 3 | 0 | 187 | 70 | 62.33 | – | 3 | 1 | – |
| 1942–3 | 2 | 4 | 0 | 148 | 58 | 37.00 | – | 2 | – | – |
| 1943–4 | 2 | 3 | 0 | 100 | 55 | 33.33 | – | 1 | – | 1 |
| 1944–5 | 4 | 7 | 0 | 348 | 125 | 49.71 | 2 | 1 | 4 | 1 |
| 1945–6 | 2 | 4 | 1 | 397 | 314* | 132.33 | 1 | – | 5 | 2 |
| 1946–7 | 2 | 4 | 0 | 88 | 42 | 22.00 | – | – | 1 | – |
| 1947–8 | 6 | 10 | 2 | 275 | 120 | 34.37 | 1 | – | 14 | 5 |
| 1948–9 India, Pakistan, Ceylon | 15 | 22 | 4 | 1,366 | 152 | 75.88 | 5 | 7 | 24 | 3 |

*(continued)*

# First-class record (batting and fielding) (Continued)

| Year | M | I | NO | Runs | HS | Ave | 100 | 50 | ct | st |
|---|---|---|---|---|---|---|---|---|---|---|
| 1949–50 | 2 | 3 | 1 | 293 | 211* | 146.50 | 1 | 1 | 3 | – |
| 1950 England | 25 | 36 | 6 | 1,674 | 168* | 55.80 | 7 | 5 | 30 | 18 |
| 1950–1 | 2 | 4 | 0 | 409 | 209 | 102.25 | 1 | 2 | 1 | – |
| 1951–2 Australia, New Zealand | 13 | 23 | 1 | 1,098 | 186 | 49.90 | 4 | 6 | 12 | 3 |
| 1952–3 | 6 | 8 | 1 | 508 | 125 | 72.57 | 2 | 2 | 9 | – |
| 1953 England | 2 | 4 | 0 | 141 | 115 | 35.25 | 1 | – | 4 | – |
| 1953–4 | 6 | 12 | 2 | 723 | 220 | 72.30 | 3 | 3 | 4 | – |
| 1954 England | 1 | 2 | 1 | 42 | 39* | 42.00 | – | – | – | – |
| 1954–5 | 7 | 13 | 0 | 962 | 155 | 74.00 | 5 | 4 | 5 | – |
| 1955–6 | 3 | 4 | 0 | 149 | 130 | 37.25 | 1 | – | 2 | – |
| 1956–7 | 2 | 2 | 0 | 90 | 64 | 45.00 | – | 1 | 4 | – |
| 1957 England | 21 | 36 | 5 | 1414 | 131 | 45.61 | 3 | 7 | 28 | – |
| 1957–8 | 5 | 6 | 1 | 414 | 145 | 82.80 | 1 | 2 | 4 | – |
| 1958–9 | 2 | 4 | 1 | 195 | 70 | 65.00 | – | 2 | 2 | – |
| 1959–60 | 4 | 6 | 1 | 277 | 83 | 55.40 | – | 3 | 5 | – |
| 1960–1 | 1 | 2 | 1 | 154 | 108 | 154.00 | 1 | – | – | – |
| 1961–2 | 3 | 5 | 1 | 90 | 60 | 22.50 | – | 1 | 6 | – |
| 1962–3 | 1 | 2 | 0 | 17 | 13 | 8.50 | – | – | 3 | – |
| 1963–4 | 4 | 7 | 0 | 271 | 105 | 38.71 | 1 | 1 | 3 | – |
| Total | 146 | 238 | 29 | 11,838 | 314* | 56.64 | 40 | 54 | 174 | 33 |

*Not out

# First-class record (bowling)

| Year | O | M | R | w | Ave | Best | 5wi |
|---|---|---|---|---|---|---|---|
| 1942 | 5 | 0 | 20 | 0 | – | – | – |
| 1942–3 | 4 | 0 | 24 | 1 | 24.00 | 1/24 | – |
| 1943–4 | 4.7 | 0 | 12 | 1 | 12.00 | 1/1 | – |
| 1946–7 | 6 | 2 | 7 | 0 | – | – | – |
| 1947–8 | 3 | 2 | 2 | 0 | – | – | – |
| 1948–9 India, Pakistan, Ceylon | 63 | 18 | 130 | 1 | 130.00 | 1/26 | – |
| 1949–50 | 50.3 | 11 | 124 | 8 | 15.50 | 4/26 | – |
| 1950 England | 12 | 6 | 22 | 0 | – | – | – |
| 1950–1 | 13 | 5 | 29 | 0 | – | – | – |
| 1951–2 Australia, New Zealand | 8 | 3 | 8 | 1 | 8.00 | 1/8 | – |
| 1952–3 | 61 | 26 | 88 | 2 | 44.00 | 2/12 | – |
| 1953 England | 4 | 0 | 13 | 0 | – | – | – |
| 1953–4 | 83.3 | 38 | 159 | 8 | 19.87 | 4/42 | – |
| 1954–5 | 72 | 24 | 156 | 4 | 39.00 | 3/50 | – |
| 1955–6 | 50 | 14 | 116 | 3 | 38.66 | 1/15 | – |
| 1956–7 | 4 | 2 | 2 | 0 | – | – | – |
| 1957 England | 8 | 2 | 28 | 0 | – | – | – |
| 1957–8 | 23 | 10 | 29 | 0 | – | – | – |
| 1958–9 | 19.3 | 2 | 68 | 0 | – | – | – |
| 1959–60 | 38 | 8 | 114 | 1 | 114.00 | 1/43 | – |
| 1961–2 | 7 | 3 | 12 | 0 | – | – | – |
| 1963–4 | 35.1 | 8 | 106 | 5 | 21.20 | 5/41 | 1 |
| **Total** | **574.5** | **184** | **1,269** | **35** | **36.25** | **5/41** | **1** |

## Test record (batting and fielding)

| Season | Opponent | M | I | NO | Runs | HS | Ave | 100 | 50 | ct | st |
|--------|----------|---|---|----|----|------|-----|-----|----|----|-----|
| 1947–8 | England | 4 | 7 | 1 | 133 | 45 | 22.16 | 0 | 0 | 11 | 5 |
| 1948–9 | India | 5 | 7 | 0 | 452 | 152 | 64.57 | 2 | 2 | 9 | 2 |
| 1950 | England | 4 | 6 | 1 | 229 | 168* | 45.80 | 1 | 0 | 4 | 3 |
| 1951–2 | Australia | 3 | 6 | 0 | 87 | 60 | 14.50 | 0 | 1 | 4 | 1 |
| 1951–2 | New Zealand | 2 | 3 | 0 | 199 | 115 | 66.33 | 1 | 1 | 2 | – |
| 1952–3 | India | 5 | 7 | 1 | 457 | 125 | 76.16 | 2 | 1 | 7 | – |
| 1953–4 | England | 5 | 10 | 2 | 698 | 220 | 87.25 | 3 | 3 | 3 | – |
| 1954–5 | Australia | 5 | 10 | 0 | 827 | 155 | 82.70 | 5 | 2 | 5 | – |
| 1957 | England | 5 | 10 | 1 | 247 | 90 | 27.44 | 0 | 1 | 3 | – |
| 1957–8 | Pakistan | 4 | 5 | 1 | 385 | 145 | 96.25 | 1 | 2 | 3 | – |
| 1959–60 | England | 2 | 3 | 0 | 84 | 53 | 28.00 | 0 | 1 | 2 | – |
| **Total** | | **44** | **74** | **7** | **3,798** | **220** | **56.68** | **15** | **14** | **53** | **11** |

## Test record (bowling)

| Season | Opponent | O | M | R | w | Ave | Best | 5wi |
|---|---|---|---|---|---|---|---|---|
| 1948–9 | India | 3 | 0 | 12 | 0 | – | – | – |
| 1950 | England | 4 | 1 | 12 | 0 | – | – | – |
| 1952–3 | India | 35 | 14 | 48 | 2 | 24.00 | 2/12 | – |
| 1953–4 | England | 53 | 24 | 94 | 4 | 23.50 | 3/52 | – |
| 1954–5 | Australia | 71 | 24 | 152 | 4 | 38.00 | 3/50 | – |
| 1957 | England | 1 | 0 | 4 | 0 | – | – | – |
| 1957–8 | Pakistan | 12 | 5 | 16 | 0 | – | – | – |
| 1959–60 | England | 20 | 4 | 70 | 1 | 70.00 | 1/43 | – |
| **Total** | | **199** | **72** | **408** | **11** | **37.09** | **3/50** | – |

## First-class centuries

| 1. | October 1944 | 125 | Barbados v. British Guiana | Bourda |
|---|---|---|---|---|
| 2. | February 1945 | 103 | Barbados v. Trinidad | Queen's Park Oval |
| 3. | February 1946 | 314 | Barbados v. Trinidad | Queen's Park Oval |
| 4. | January 1948 | 120 | Barbados v. MCC | Kensington Oval |
| 5. | November 1948 | 152 | WEST INDIES v. INDIA* | New Delhi |
| 6. | November 1948 | 129 | West Indians v. West Zone | Poona |
| 7. | December 1948 | 108 | WEST INDIES v. INDIA | Calcutta |
| 8. | January 1949 | 120 | West Indians v. Governor of Bihar's XI | Jamshedpur |

*(continued)*

# First-class centuries (Continued)

| | | | | |
|---|---|---|---|---|
| 9. | February 1949 | 125 | West Indians v. Ceylon | Colombo |
| 10. | February 1950 | 211 | Barbados v. British Guiana | Kensington Oval |
| 11. | May 1950 | 128 | West Indians v. Surrey | Kennington Oval |
| 12. | May 1950 | 117 | West Indians v. Somerset | Taunton |
| 13. | June 1950 | 168 | WEST INDIES v. ENGLAND | Lord's |
| 14. | July 1950 | 149 | West Indians v. Surrey | Kennington Oval |
| 15. | August 1950 | 126 | West Indians v. Gloucestershire | Cheltenham |
| 16. | September 1950 | 103 | West Indians v. South of England | Hastings |
| 17. | September 1950 | 121 | West Indians v. Mr H. D. G. Leveson-Gower's XI | Scarborough |
| 18. | March 1951 | 209 | Barbados v. Trinidad | Kensington Oval |
| 19. | January 1952 | 186 | West Indians v. Tasmania | Hobart |
| 20. | January 1952 | 105 | West Indians v. Victoria | Melbourne |
| 21. | February 1952 | 115 | West Indians v. New Zealand | Auckland |
| 22. | February 1952 | 148 | West Indians v. Wellington | Wellington |
| 23. | March 1953 | 125 | WEST INDIES v. INDIA | Bourda |
| 24. | April 1953 | 118 | WEST INDIES v. INDIA | Sabina Park |

## First-class centuries  (Continued)

| 25. | June 1953 | 115 | Commonwealth XI v. Essex | Romford |
|---|---|---|---|---|
| 26. | February 1954 | 220 | WEST INDIES v. ENGLAND | Kensington Oval |
| 27. | March 1954 | 124 | WEST INDIES v. ENGLAND | Queen's Park Oval |
| 28. | March 1954 | 116 | WEST INDIES v. ENGLAND | Sabina Park |
| 29. | March 1955 | 108 | WEST INDIES v. AUSTRALIA | Sabina Park |
| 30. | April 1955 | 126 | WEST INDIES v. AUSTRALIA | Queen's Park Oval |
| 31. | April 1955 | 110 | WEST INDIES v. AUSTRALIA | Queen's Park Oval |
| 32. | June 1955 | 155 | WEST INDIES v. AUSTRALIA | Sabina Park |
| 33. | June 1955 | 110 | WEST INDIES v. AUSTRALIA | Sabina Park |
| 34. | March 1956 | 130 | Barbados v. E. W. Swanton's XI | Kensington Oval |
| 35. | May 1957 | 117 | West Indians v. MCC | Lord's |
| 36. | May 1957 | 115 | West Indians v. Nottinghamshire | Trent Bridge |
| 37. | August 1957 | 131 | West Indians v. Kent | Canterbury |
| 38. | March 1958 | 145 | WEST INDIES v. PAKISTAN | Bourda |
| 39. | April 1961 | 108 | British Guiana v. E. W. Swanton's XI | Bourda |
| 40. | September 1963 | 105 | F. M. M. Worrell's XI v. C. C. Hunte's XI | Sabina Park |

*Matches in capital letters denotes Test matches

# Record for Enfield in the Lancashire League

| (Batting) | | | | |
|---|---|---|---|---|
| *Season* | | *NO* | *Runs* | *Ave* |
| 1951 | 23 | 7 | 1,136 | 71.00 |
| 1952 | 20 | 8 | 955 | 79.58 |
| 1953 | 21 | 10 | 1,117 | 101.54 |
| 1954 | 19 | 5 | 783 | 55.92 |
| TOTAL | **83** | **30** | **3,991** | **75.30** |

| (Bowling) | | | | | |
|---|---|---|---|---|---|
| *Season* | *O* | *M* | *R* | *W* | *Ave* |
| 1951 | 303.3 | | 1,032 | 53 | 19.47 |
| 1952 | 215.3 | | 710 | 44 | 16.13 |
| 1953 | 260 | | 707 | 52 | 13.59 |
| 1954 | 233.3 | | 511 | 72 | 7.09 |
| **TOTAL** | **1,012.1** | | **2,960** | **221** | **13.39** |

# Notes

## INTRODUCTION

1 Timothy Arlott, *John Arlott: A Memoir* (London: Pan, 1995), p. 74.

## CHAPTER 1: EARLY YEARS – AND FIRST-CLASS CRICKET

1 Clyde Walcott, *Sixty Years on the Back Foot* (London: Orion, 2000), p. 2.
2 Ibid.
3 Ibid.
4 Ibid., p. 7.
5 Ibid.
6 Keith Sandiford, *Cricket Nurseries of Colonial Barbados: The Elite Schools, 1865–1966* (Kingston, Jamaica: University of the West Indies Press 1990), p. 3.
7 Clyde Walcott, *Island Cricketers* (London: Hodder & Stoughton, 1958), p. 15.
8 Ivo Tennant, *Frank Worrell* (Cambridge: Lutterworth, 1987), p. 8.
9 Frank Worrell, *Cricket Punch* (London: Stanley Paul, 1959), p. 25.
10 Walcott, *Island Cricketers*, p. 17.
11 Ibid.

# Notes

12 Ibid., p. 15.
13 Ibid., p. 26.
14 Ibid.
15 Ibid., p. 27.
16 Ibid.
17 Ibid., p. 28.
18 Ibid.
19 Ibid., p. 30.
20 Ibid.
21 Ibid.

## CHAPTER 2: WEST INDIES HERO

1 Clyde Walcott, *Sixty Years on the Back Foot* (London: Orion, 2000), p. 23.
2 Clyde Walcott, *Island Cricketers* (London: Hodder & Stoughton, 1958), p. 33.
3 Ibid., p. 32.
4 Ibid., p. 34.
5 Ibid., p. 35.
6 Ibid., p. 36.
7 Ibid., p. 43.
8 'Sir Clyde Walcott', *The Times*, 28 August 2006.
9 C. L. R. James, *Beyond a Boundary* (London: Yellow Jersey, 2005), p. 303.
10 Michael Manley, *A History of West Indies Cricket* (London: Andre Deutsch, 2002), p. 68.
11 Jeff Stollmeyer, *Everything Under the Sun* (London: Stanley Paul, 1983), p. 116.
12 Frank Worrell, *Cricket Punch* (London: Stanley Paul, 1959), p. 127.
13 Interview with the author, 2023.
14 Everton Weekes, foreword in Clyde Walcott, *Sixty Years on the Back Foot* (London: Orion, 2000), p. vii.
15 Simon Lister, *Fire in Babylon* (London: Yellow Jersey, 2016), p. 347.
16 Ibid.
17 Written, it appears, by Lord Kitchener, but popularised by Lord Beginner.

# Notes

18  Walcott, *Island Cricketers*, p. 53.

19  Ibid., p. 9.

20  John Arlott, *Basingstoke Boy* ( London: Willow, 1990), p. 196.

21  'Sir Clyde Walcott on the West Indies' First Win at Lord's', *Sporting Witness*, BBC Sounds, www.bbc.co.uk/sounds/play/poojndzy

22  Ibid.

23  Walcott, *Island Cricketers*, p. 39.

24  Ibid., p. 56.

25  Andrea Stuart, *Sugar in the Blood* (London: Portobello, 2013), p. 344.

26  Ibid., p. 345.

27  Ibid.

28  Walcott, *Sixty Years on the Back Foot*, p. 44.

29  Ibid.

30  Ernest Eytle, *Frank Worrell* (London: Sportsmans Book Club, 1965), p. 117.

31  Walcott, *Island Cricketers*, p. 63.

32  Stollmeyer, *Everything Under the Sun*, p. 56.

33  Ibid.

## Chapter 3: India, Enfield and the Hutton tour

1  Interview with the author, 2023.

2  Ibid.

3  Michael Manley, *A History of West Indies Cricket* (London: Andre Deutsch, 2002), p. 104.

4  Ernest Eytle, *Frank Worrell* (London: Sportsmans Book Club, 1965), p. 124.

5  Clyde Walcott, *Island Cricketers* (London: Hodder & Stoughton, 1958), p. 83.

6  Clyde Walcott, *Sixty Years on the Back Foot* (London: Orion, 2000), p. 49.

7  Ibid., p. 50.

8  Quoted in Walcott, *Sixty Years on the Back Foot*, p. 62.

9  Walcott, *Sixty Years on the Back Foot*, p. 63.

10  Ibid.

11  Ibid., p. 50.

12  Ibid.
13  Ibid., p. 60.
14  In *Cricket in the Leagues* (London: Eyre & Spottiswoode, 1970, p. 97) author John Kay picked Walcott in his greatest ever Lancashire League XI.

## CHAPTER 4: TO BRITISH GUIANA

1  *Daily Argosy*, 17 October 1954.
2  Quoted in Clem Seecharan, *From Ranji to Rohan* (Hertford: Hansib, 2009), p. 119.
3  Ibid., p. 24.
4  Clem Seecharan, *Tiger in the Stars* (London: Macmillan, 1997), p. 14.
5  *Sunderland Echo*, 29 April 1954.
6  Clyde Walcott, *Island Cricketers* (London: Hodder & Stoughton, 1958), p. 100.
7  Ibid.
8  Ibid.
9  Interview with the author, 2023.
10  Ibid.
11  Ibid.
12  Ibid.
13  Ibid.
14  Clyde Walcott, *Sixty Years on the Back Foot* (London: Orion, 2000), p. 64.
15  Ibid., p. 65.
16  Walcott, *Island Cricketers*, p. 100.
17  Seecharan, *From Ranji to Rohan*, p. 153.
18  Ibid., p. 121.
19  Frank Birbalsingh and Clem Seecharan, *Indo-Westindian Cricket* (Hertford: Hansib, 1988), p. 109.
20  Ibid., p. 125.
21  Seecharan, *From Ranji to Rohan*, p. 97.
22  Garfield Sobers and J. S. Barker (eds), *Cricket in the Sun: A History of West Indies Cricket* (London: Arthur Barker, 1967), p. 45.
23  Interview with the author, 2023.
24  Ibid.

# Notes

25 Seecharan, *From Ranji to Rohan*, p. 115.

26 Ibid., p. 121.

27 Clem Seecharan, *Joe Solomon and the Spirit of Port Mourant* (Hertford: Hansib, 2022), p. 58.

28 Seecharan, *From Ranji to Rohan*, p. 120.

29 Walcott, *Sixty Years on the Back Foot*, p. 67.

30 Seecharan, *From Ranji to Rohan*, p. 124.

31 Walcott, *Island Cricketers*, p. 176.

32 *Booker News*, 16 August 1963.

33 Seecharan, *Joe Solomon and the Spirit of Port Mourant*, p. 111.

34 Walcott, *Sixty Years on the Back Foot*, p. 67.

## CHAPTER 5: REACHING A PEAK – AND RETIREMENT

1 Michael Manley, *A History of West Indies Cricket* (London: Andre Deutsch, 2002), p. 118.

2 Clyde Walcott, *Island Cricketers* (London: Hodder & Stoughton, 1958), p. 104.

3 Ibid.

4 Ibid.

5 Ivo Tennant, *Frank Worrell* (Cambridge: Lutterworth, 1987), p. 108.

6 Clyde Walcott, *Sixty Years on the Back Foot* (London: Orion, 2000), p. 72.

7 Frank Worrell, *Cricket Punch* (London: Stanley Paul, 1959), p. 128.

8 Interview with the author, 2023.

9 David Woodhouse, *Who Only Cricket Know* (London: Fairfield, 2021), p. 348.

10 Manley, *A History of West Indies Cricket*, p. 108.

11 Ibid.

12 Woodhouse, *Who Only Cricket Know*, p. 354.

13 Walcott, *Sixty Years on the Back Foot*, p. 77.

14 Ibid.

15 *The Civil and Military Gazette*, 31 July 1957, p. 11.

16 Walcott, *Sixty Years on the Back Foot*, p. 77.

17 Ivo Tennant, *Frank Worrell* (Cambridge: Lutterworth, 1987), p. 45.

# Notes

18 John Arlott, *Basingstoke Boy* (London: Willow, 1990), p. 270.

19 Ibid.

20 Manley, *A History of West Indies Cricket*, p. 129.

21 Walcott, *Sixty Years on the Back Foot*, p. 87.

22 Ibid.

23 Clem Seecharan, *Joe Solomon and the Spirit of Port Mourant* (Hertford: Hansib, 2022), p. 159.

24 Ibid.

25 Ibid.

26 Ibid., p. 242.

27 Ibid.

28 Mike Coward, *Calypso Summer* (Australia: ABC Books, 2000), p. 64.

29 Frank Birbalsingh and Clem Seecharan, *Indo-Westindian Cricket* (Hertford: Hansib, 1988), p. 122.

30 C. L. R. James, *Beyond a Boundary* (London: Yellow Jersey, 2005), p. 306.

31 Ibid.

32 Ibid.

33 Ibid.

34 Walcott, *Sixty Years on the Back Foot*, p. 68.

35 Ibid.

36 James, *Beyond a Boundary*, p. 233.

37 Ibid.

38 Birbalsingh and Seecharan, *Indo-Westindian Cricket*, p. 122.

39 Ibid.

40 *Booker News*, 16 August 1963.

## CHAPTER 6: STEERING THE WEST INDIES TO GREATNESS

1 Clyde Walcott, *Sixty Years on the Back Foot* (London: Orion, 2000), p. 90.

2 Ibid., p. 92.

3 Ibid.

4 Ibid., p. 89.

5 Ibid., p. 95.

6 Ibid., p. 92.

7 Ibid., p. 98.

8 Ibid., p. 99.

# Notes

9   Ibid.

10  Simon Lister, *Supercat* (Bath: Fairfield, 2007), p. 80.

11  Ibid.

12  Walcott, *Sixty Years on the Back Foot*, p. 101.

13  Ibid.

14  Ibid., p. 100.

15  Preston, Norman, *Wisden Almanack 1975*, at www.espncricinfo.com/wisdenalmanack/content/story/150279.html

16  Walcott, *Sixty Years on the Back Foot*, p. 104.

17  Simon Lister, *Fire in Babylon* (London: Yellow Jersey, 2016), p. 55.

18  Walcott, *Sixty Years on the Back Foot*, p. 113.

19  Ibid.

20  Interview with the author, 2023.

21  Ibid.

22  Ibid.

23  Ibid.

24  Walcott, *Sixty Years on the Back Foot*, p. 116.

25  Ibid.

26  Ibid., p. 123.

27  Ibid.

28  Interview with the author, 2023.

29  Ibid.

30  Walcott, *Sixty Years on the Back Foot*, p. 127.

31  Ibid.

32  Ibid., p. 109.

33  Ibid., p. 130.

34  *Daily Mirror*, 5 May 1980.

35  Walcott's off-field duties included helping the TV personality Eamonn Andrews ambush Lloyd for the BBC's *This is Your Life* programme at the Commonwealth Institute building in London. Telling Lloyd that they had a function to attend there, he ordered them both a taxi – but needed to make sure the driver executed a couple of extra turns around the block when he spotted a host of giveaway celebrity guests arriving outside the venue.

36  Walcott, *Sixty Years on the Back Foot*, p. 129.

# Notes

Greenidge, *The Man in the Middle* (Newton Abbott: David & Charles, 1980), p. 77.
38 Walcott, *Sixty Years on the Back Foot*, p. 132.
39 Ibid., p. 134.
40 Ibid.
41 Michael Manley, *A History of West Indies Cricket* (London: Andre Deutsch, 2002), p. 404.
42 Interview with the author, 2023.
43 Ibid.
44 Walcott, *Sixty Years on the Back Foot*, p. 156.
45 Interview with the author, 2023.
46 Ibid.
47 Ibid., p. 154.
48 Ibid., p. 157.
49 Ibid.
50 Ibid., p. 104.
51 Ibid.
52 Ibid., p. 105.
53 David Woodhouse, *Who Only Cricket Know* (London: Fairfield, 2021), p. 373.
54 Ibid.
55 Walcott, *Sixty Years on the Back Foot*, p. 117.
56 Ibid.
57 Ibid.
58 Ibid., p. 118.
59 Ibid.
60 Ibid.
61 Ibid., p. 152.
62 Ibid.
63 Manley, *A History of West Indies Cricket*, p. 405.

## Chapter 7: ICC and beyond

1 Clyde Walcott, *Sixty Years on the Back Foot* (London: Orion, 2000), p. 179.
2 Interview with Hilary Beckles in *The Development of West Indies Cricket Vol 1* (Barbados: The Press, University of the West Indies, 1998), p. 186.

# Notes

3 Michael Manley, *A History of West Indies Cricket* (London: Andre Deutsch, 2002), p. 404.

4 Interview with Hilary Beckles, p. 187.

5 Ibid.

6 Ivo Tennant, *Frank Worrell* (Cambridge: Lutterworth, 1987), p. 1.

7 Walcott, *Sixty Years on the Back Foot*, p. 11.

8 www.espncricinfo.com/story/weekes-leads-the-tributes-257901

9 Ibid.

10 Ibid.

11 http://news.bbc.co.uk/sport1/hi/cricket/other_international/west_indies/5289258.stm

12 Ibid.

13 *Weekend Nation*, 24 January 2020, p. 19.

## CHAPTER 8: AN ASSESSMENT

1 Simon Lister, *Fire in Babylon* (London: Yellow Jersey, 2016), p. 323.

2 Clyde Walcott, *Island Cricketers* (London: Hodder & Stoughton, 1958), p. 181.

3 *Daily Mail*, 28 August 2006, p. 62.

4 Michael Manley, *A History of West Indies Cricket* (London: Andre Deutsch, 2002), p. 404.

5 Clem Seecharan, *Joe Solomon and the Spirit of Port Mourant* (Hertford: Hansib, 2022), p. 55.

6 Interview with the author, 2023.

7 Interview with Hilary Beckles in *The Development of West Indies Cricket Vol 1* (Barbados: The Press, University of the West Indies 1998), p. 193.

# Bibliography

Arlott, John, *Arlott on Cricket: His Writings on the Game* (London: Willow, 1984).

Arlott, John, *Basingstoke Boy* (London: Willow, 1990).

Arlott, Timothy, *John Arlott: A Memoir* (London: Pan, 1995).

Babb, Colin, *They Gave the Crowd Plenty Fun* (Hertford: Hansib, 2012).

Baksh, Vaneisa, *Son of Grace: Frank Worrell – A Biography* (London: Fairfield, 2023).

Beckles, Hilary, *The Development of West Indies Cricket Vol 1* (Barbados: The Press, University of the West Indies, 1998).

Beckles, Hilary, *The Development of West Indies Cricket Vol 2* (Barbados: The Press, University of the West Indies, 1998).

Birbalsingh, Frank and Seecharan, Clem, *Indo-Westindian Cricket* (Hertford: Hansib, 1988).

Coward, Mike, *Calypso Summer* (Australia: ABC Books, 2000).

Dalrymple, Henderson, *50 Great West Indian Cricketers* (Hertford: Hansib, 1983).

Eytle, Ernest, *Frank Worrell* (London: Sportsmans Book Club, 1965).

Greenidge, Gordon, *The Man in the Middle* (Newton Abbott: David & Charles, 1980).

James, C. L. R., *Cricket* (London: Allison & Busby, 1989).

# Bibliography

James, C. L. R., *Beyond a Boundary* (London: Yellow Jersey, 2005).

James, C. L. R., *A Majestic Innings* (London: Aurum, 2006).

Kay, John, *Cricket in the Leagues* (London: Eyre & Spottiswoode, 1970).

Lawrence, Bridgette, *100 Great West Indian Cricketers* (Hertford: Hansib, 1988).

Lister, Simon, *Supercat* (Bath: Fairfield, 2007).

Lister, Simon, *Fire in Babylon* (London: Yellow Jersey, 2016).

Manley, Michael, *A History of West Indies Cricket* (London: Andre Deutsch, 2002).

Mason, Peter, *Learie Constantine* (London: Macmillan, 2008).

Murtagh, Andrew, *Gentleman and Player* (Worthing: Pitch, 2017).

Nicole, Christopher, *West Indian Cricket* (London: Phoenix Sports, 1957).

Richards, Viv, *Sir Vivian: The Definitive Autobiography* (London: Michael Joseph, 2001).

Sandiford, Keith, *Cricket Nurseries of Colonial Barbados: The Elite Schools, 1865–1966* (Kingston, Jamaica: The University of the West Indies Press, 1990).

Seecharan, Clem, *Tiger in the Stars* (London: Macmillan, 1997).

Seecharan, Clem, *Sweetening Bitter Sugar* (Kingston, Jamaica: Ian Randle, 2005).

Seecharan, Clem, *Muscular Learning* (Kingston, Jamaica: Ian Randle, 2006).

Seecharan, Clem, *From Ranji to Rohan* (Hertford: Hansib, 2009).

Seecharan, Clem, *Joe Solomon and the Spirit of Port Mourant* (Hertford: Hansib, 2022).

Sobers, Garfield and Barker, J. S., *Cricket in the Sun: A History of West Indies Cricket* (London: Arthur Barker, 1967).

Stollmeyer, Jeff, *Everything Under the Sun* (London: Stanley Paul, 1983).

Stoute, Deborah, Miller, Carmen, and Beckles, Hilary, *Celebrating the 3W's – A Legacy of West Indian Cricket* (Barbados: The 3W's Celebration Committee, 2003).

Stuart, Andrea, *Sugar in the Blood* (London: Portobello, 2013).

# Bibliography

Tennant, Ivo, *Frank Worrell: A Biography* (Cambridge: Lutterworth, 1987).

Walcott, Clyde, *Island Cricketers* (London: Hodder & Stoughton, 1958).

Walcott, Clyde, *Sixty Years on the Back Foot* (London: Orion, 2000).

Worrell, Frank, *Cricket Punch* (London: Stanley Paul, 1959).

Woodhouse, David, *Who Only Cricket Know* (London: Fairfield, 2021).

# Index

# Index

# Index

# Index

# Index

# Index

# Index

# Index